Living God's Word

Living God's Word

Reflections on the Sunday Readings
for Year A

Archbishop Terrence Prendergast

NOVALIS

Cover design and layout: Audrey Wells
Cover art: "Evangelista Matteo" - mosaico realizzato dalla Scuola Mosaicisti del Friuli (Spilimbergo PN - Italia), a.s. 1960/1961, bozzetto di Padre Leo Coppens ["Matthew the Evangelist" - mosaic created by The School of Mosaic of Friuli (Spilimbergo, PN - Italy), 1960/1961, sketch by Fr. Leo Coppens]

Published by Novalis

Publishing Office
10 Lower Spadina Avenue, Suite 400
Toronto, Ontario, Canada
M5V 2Z2

Head Office
4475 Frontenac Street
Montréal, Québec, Canada
H2H 2S2

www.novalis.ca

Cataloguing in Publication is available from Library and Archives Canada.

Printed in Canada.

We acknowledge the financial support of the Government of Canada through the Book Publishing Industry Development Program (BPIDP) for our publishing activities.

5   4   3   2   1   14   13   12   11   10

Dedication

To Cardinal Aloysius Matthew Ambrozic

"It is enough for the disciple to be like the teacher..."
(Matthew 10.25)

Acknowledgements

Over a ten-year period, it was my privilege to write a weekly set of reflections on the Sunday readings ("God's Word on Sunday") in the Toronto-based Catholic newspaper, *The Catholic Register.*

On several occasions, friends and associates suggested that these be made available in book form as an aid to those who have the challenge of providing homiletical reflections for parish and other faith communities. I have also been told that liturgy committees and study groups that gather to pray over the Scriptures in preparation for their participation in the Sunday Eucharist appreciate these reflections.

Joseph Sinasac of Novalis, who was my editor at the *Register,* prodded me to select the best of my earlier work and to write new reflections to cover any gaps in the columns caused either by an early start to Lent or by the late resumption of continuous readings after Pentecost. I am grateful for his encouragement and his patience.

My thanks go, too, to Anne Louise Mahoney, whose competent, efficient and speedy work in copy editing brought consistency, harmony and clarity to a text that had gestated over a number of years.

The present collection of readings from the liturgical year of Matthew (designated "Year A" in lectionaries) has been supplemented with reflections on solemnities that occasionally displace the Sundays of Ordinary Time.

As I commend this aid to Sunday worship to disciples aspiring to deepen their knowledge and love of the Scriptures, I am conscious of my own debt to teachers and ministers of the word who have helped me.

My Jesuit confreres from Regis College – Fathers Scott Lewis, Michael Kolarcik, Roderick A.F. Mackenzie (+1994), Joseph Plevnik (+2010) and David Michael Stanley (+1996) – have helped me immensely, as have scholar friends in the Catholic Biblical Association of America, whose annual convention was always a joy, and the scholarly communities where I spent refreshing sabbatical years: the Pontifical Biblical Institute in Rome (1987–88) and the École biblique in Jerusalem (1994–1995). May these associates rejoice in seeing ideas and expressions I have gleaned from their academic labours being handed on. Any inadequacy in transmitting their research remains entirely my own responsibility.

This work is dedicated in homage to Cardinal Aloysius Ambrozic, my *Doktorvater* (doctoral dissertation director), in the year he celebrates his 80th birthday. His encouragement of my ministry of reading, praying, studying, preaching and teaching God's word is a blessing I shall always cherish.

+Terrence Prendergast, S.J.
Archbishop of Ottawa
Feast of St. Ignatius Loyola
July 31, 2010

Contents

Foreword

The liturgical life of the Catholic Church was enriched when Vatican II, in reforming the liturgy, asked that "there should be more abundant, varied and appropriate readings from sacred Scripture". The hope of the Council was that "the treasures of the Bible should be opened more lavishly so that richer fare might be provided at the table of God's Word". This was to be an organic development fully in continuity with the practice of the Church from earliest times; now the amount of Scripture read during the celebration of the Mass would be much increased and would better express the sacred mysteries being remembered and made present.

Yet it has been a common experience that the potential this offered for enabling the kind of biblical preaching called for by the liturgy has not always been realized. Under the pressure of pastoral work, the priest or deacon could too easily end up with little more than a retelling of Gospel incidents and a moralistic reflection on them. At times, the preacher has read the Scripture passages too exclusively in light of historical/critical approaches, ignoring the essential contexts of sacred Tradition, the Church's magisterium and her life and worship. On occasion, preachers have proposed diminished or even incorrect interpretations of the sacred text.

Awareness of this situation has led to the provision of various aids for biblical homilies. Among all of them, this book by the Archbishop of Ottawa, the Most Reverend Terrence Prendergast, SJ, must have pride of place. It is a reliable resource authored by a respected biblical scholar, a work of solid but unobtrusive scholarship that offers brief but substantial exegesis of the biblical readings for Sundays and feast days. With the lectionary, with this book, with a reputable biblical commentary, as Archbishop Prendergast suggests, and with prayerful reflection, the preacher can become truly a minister of the Word.

The Gospel readings considered in the book are chiefly from the Gospel of Saint Matthew, which Archbishop Prendergast describes in his Introduction as "an invitation to confess in both word and deed that Jesus is Lord.... Matthew's is the Gospel of the risen cosmic Christ who fulfills all messianic expectations through the event of his death and resurrection". Christ is the centre and goal of history, to whom we must look and find him where he enters that history. The Christian faith rests essentially on the fact that Christ lived, died and rose again two thousand years ago in Palestine. It is he who, in the words of Saint Irenaeus, "brought eternal newness to the earth by bringing himself", and is with us today as the vital subject of the Church's liturgy. If we wish God to enter our hearts, we must hear him speak across the centuries; we realize, though, that he has already spoken in the Scriptures and that he continues to speak through them. His words, as Saint Gregory the Great tells us, reveal to us God's very heart: "Learn from the heart of God in the words of God".

The Gospels present Jesus of Nazareth to us as the Word who is God and who took on our human nature for the salvation of humankind. Jesus was therefore fully aware of this mystery and of his mission in making it known to all peoples. Yet such a mystery could not be revealed directly and without preparation to people whose minds were not ready for such doctrine. There had to be a period of maturation, a pedagogy by which especially unreceptive hearers could be helped to grasp what had been made explicit only to the little band of the apostles. These revelations could be grasped by the wider circle of disciples only when they had been made able to understand them by the events of Easter and the sending of the Holy Spirit at Pentecost. That is what we see happening in the Gospels; that is what the present book takes account of as it provides an entry to the divine pedagogy that leads the reader to Jesus of Nazareth as he was in all his reality: Son of Man and Son of God, God himself, knowing who he was and proclaiming it.

Archbishop Prendergast has given us a book that can allow us to read the Word of God with new eyes, not seeing just a precious document of the past but also a living page of actual history. It is a page always open that enables us to "taste the sweetness of the Word of God" (Hebrews 6:5) by living it in the Church, by celebrating it in the liturgy and by proclaiming it to all who will listen, making present in a personal way the words of Jesus the Incarnate Word.

Francis Cardinal George, OMI
Archbishop of Chicago

Introduction

The Year of Matthew and Solemnities

In this volume, the background reflections for the Sunday scriptural readings are taken from the liturgical year designated by the letter "A", which features continuous readings from the Gospel of Matthew. Several Sundays after Christmas, during Lent and in Eastertide are taken from the Gospel of John; this also happens in Year B, which is devoted mainly to Mark's Gospel, and in Year C, when selections are taken primarily from the Gospel of Luke.

As a supplement to these reflections on Year A, a similar series of reflections is provided for those Solemnities of Our Lord, the Blessed Virgin Mary and important feasts of saints that – outside of Advent, Lent and Easter – can displace the Sunday celebration in Ordinary Time.

Generally speaking, the first reading, which is from the Old Testament (except in Eastertide, when selections from the Acts of the Apostles are featured), has been chosen to complement the gospel passage, by either anticipating the message of Jesus or revealing some truth about him (sometimes related as biblical prophecy to its fulfillment in Christ) or otherwise presenting similar themes to those found in the gospel.

The second reading is generally from one of the Letters of Paul or one of the other apostolic authors (James, Jude, Peter, John), and is usually read for a number of Sundays in a row (depending on the length of the letter).

Given the above configuration of scriptural readings, my reflection generally centres on the gospel reading, with references of shorter or longer length on the first reading and, usually, a brief allusion to the second reading. On occasion, because of the importance of the text or to offer a variety in the focus of the homily, my focus falls on the second reading or, less frequently still, on the psalm.

The Gospel of Matthew

Scholars remain undecided about several aspects concerning this longest of the gospels which for centuries held pride of place in the Church's teaching and life.

Mainstream scriptural interpreters place this gospel's composition towards the end of the first century (80–90 AD), possibly in a mixed Jewish-Gentile community such as was found at Antioch in Syria.

Matthew's gospel stresses that Jesus is the Son of God who fulfills what the Old Testament foretold of the Messiah (for example, "This was to fulfill what had been spoken by the Lord through the prophet, 'Out of Egypt I have called my son'" [2.15]).

Inviting the follower of Jesus to confess in both word and deed that Jesus is Lord (cf. Matthew 7.21), Matthew depicts Jesus as a prophet powerful in word and deed (4.23; 9.35).

To underline this emphasis on Jesus' words and deeds, the evangelist intersperses narrative blocks depicting Jesus' healings and miracles with five major speeches.

The Sermon on the Mount constitutes the first of the five great addresses Jesus gives (chapters 5–7). Later, Jesus shares instructions with his apostles as he sends them out on mission (chapter 10), then proclaims to them the parables of the kingdom of heaven and their meaning (chapter 13).

In chapter 18, Jesus describes how life should be lived in the Church, focusing on the need to care for vulnerable "little ones" – who are easily led astray by bad example – and on the enduring need for forgiveness among his disciples.

The climax to Jesus' instructions are found in his eschatological parables and teaching, which culminate in the Last Judgment (chapters 24–25). At the end of the ages, as the glorious Son of Man, Jesus uncovers the criterion for inheriting the Father's kingdom: what was done or not done "for the least of my brethren" (25.40, 45) was given or refused to Jesus. All will be judged on their deeds.

This gospel emphasis on "doing" has often coloured the way people interpret the message of the Beatitudes. Some people are led to think that only when they have conformed their lives to the program Jesus enunciates will they become pleasing to God. There is a risk here of getting Jesus' message backwards.

Jesus proclaims good news from God to the poor in spirit, the mourning, those who hunger and thirst for righteousness (right relations between God and humanity and among members of the human family).

Jesus declares that God has chosen to give humans, who struggle in their yearnings, the free gift of the kingdom. In this vein, one "dynamic equivalence" translation—one that attempts to give the sense of the passage rather than word-for-word equivalence—rendered the "poor in spirit" of the first beatitude as "those who know their need for God" (J.B. Phillips).

In beginning with God, all is grace, all is gift. Then comes the challenge to every person who would remain a charter member of God's household: Be what you are! Live the life of the kingdom!

The message of the Sermon on the Mount constantly oscillates between the call God makes possible ("You are the light of the world") and the challenge to live it out ("Let your light shine before others"). Putting all the onus on oneself could lead to frustration or to self-righteousness.

Yet, to do nothing but wait on God would be to fall into the error of spiritual passivity. Life in the kingdom is a partnership begun and sustained by God, but which his children rejoice in making their own. They go so far as to rejoice in suffering willingly for Jesus' sake (when people "utter all kinds of evil against you falsely on my account" [5.11]).

Matthew's is the gospel of the risen, cosmic Christ. The Messiah, son of Abraham, son of David, Son of Man, Son of God, who fulfills all messianic expectations through the cosmic event of his death and resurrection, is present in the reading or proclamation of the gospel ("for where two or three are gathered in my name, I am there among them" [18.20]).

Jesus is God's chosen, powerful in word and deed, who calls others to have a consistency between what they say and do. All disciples are moving towards the last judgment, but need not fear this occurrence, for the Lord who is to come is already with his Church ("remember, I am with you always until the end of the age" [28.20]).

Preparing for Sunday Mass

Each homilist, study group or other interpreters of the Sunday scriptures (such as those engaged in children's Liturgy of the Word) will devise their own appropriate manner of using this book. The following thoughts may help those looking for a methodology.

The most important starting point is to read through the gospel of a particular Sunday or solemnity and then the first reading several times, looking for common and differing emphases as well as any structural features that stand out.

A second point would be to list problem areas in interpretation. In the texts, which matters or issues might contemporary readers not understand? Which issues might they struggle with?

At this time, one could read the reflections on the readings to see what clarifications are offered. As each text is very brief (around 700 words), it is not likely that every difficulty will be resolved. Here we see the importance of having access to a biblical commentary or biblical dictionary. I have often found that commentators touch on every issue except the one that interests me; hence the need for several other tools.

Next, the second reading could be read meditatively, with the same pattern used in contemplating the gospel and first reading. Because all the texts for solemnities, Advent and Lent are chosen in function of the feast or liturgical season, the second reading on those occasions will more generally fit with the gospel and first reading. On the Sundays of Ordinary Time or in the Easter season, meanwhile, the second readings are continuous.

Finally, the psalm could be prayed as a closing devotional exercise that picks up a theme of the Sunday or feast day.

May Mary, Mother of the Word Incarnate, who remains for the Church the model for believers who strive to "hear the word of God and obey it" (Luke 11.28), intercede for all who will use this book to deepen their knowledge of God's self-communication in his holy word.

First Sunday of Advent

Being Ready for the Lord's Coming

* 1st reading: Isaiah 2.1-5
* Psalm: 122
* 2nd reading: Romans 13.11-14
* Gospel: Matthew 24.37-44

The word "Advent" means "coming". The season of Advent has a two-fold focus. The first part looks hopefully towards the *Parousia*, the coming of Christ in glory at the end of the ages (the First Sunday). The second phase shifts to the announcement of his coming in history as the Child born in Bethlehem (the Fourth Sunday). Between these two poles, the liturgy urges upon Christians the proper dispositions for receiving Christ at his coming by re-counting John the Baptist's heralding of Jesus, "the Coming One" (the Second and Third Sundays).

The Book of Isaiah is a pre-eminent source of Advent themes – joy, conversion, zeal for God's will – and for biblical thought about God's designs for "the Day of the Lord". In a future known only to God, an era of universal peace will be ushered in.

The prophet foretold a period when people would reshape implements of war into farming tools ("they shall beat their swords into ploughshares and their spears into pruning hooks"). This passage resonated in the modern world more than a half-century ago when the United Nations Organization was founded and adopted this vision as its aim.

Today more than ever, Isaiah's vision of peace ("nation shall not lift up sword against nation, neither shall they learn war any more") speaks to human hearts. Yet Isaiah saw peace as the fruit of meditation on God's word and a willingness to shape one's life according to divine counsels ("out of Zion shall go forth instruction, and the word of the Lord from Jerusalem").

Humanity's desire to guide their lives by God's teaching elevates "the mountain of the Lord's house" above all the world's mountains. Jerusalem then becomes a symbol of the Heavenly City where God's will rules.

The early Church saw biblical prophecy fulfilled in Jesus' passion and resurrection. Paul voiced their expectation that biblical prophecies such as Isaiah's dream of universal harmony and peace would be fulfilled in Christ's return. This would mean the completion of the process of salvation begun in his resurrection. Paul and his fellow Christians were convinced that Jesus' coming in glory would be soon ("salvation is nearer to us now than when we became believers").

Paul developed the image of the "day of the Lord", associating Christians with rejecting sinful behaviour and adopting a way of life fitting to the light ("Let us then lay aside the works of darkness and put on the armour of light").

In his *Confessions*, Augustine of Hippo tells how he let this Pauline invitation transform his life. While in Milan, he heard a child singing in a nearby house, *"Tolle lege, tolle lege"* ("Take up and read"). The parchment at his feet was this text from Romans. Letting go of his former resistance, Augustine surrendered to the graced message ("let us live honourably as in the day"; ... "put on the Lord Jesus Christ").

Jesus used the past ("the days of Noah") to shape his teaching about the coming of the Son of Man, the mysterious term he used to refer to himself. People in Noah's day, seeing him building the ark, kept about their business, unaware of the flood that would sweep them away. Only Noah and his family were ready for the day of separation between those saved and those lost.

Jesus speaks of a division that "the Coming" will produce. Of two men working in a field and two women sharing the work of grinding

·meal, "one will be taken and one will be left". It is not clear whether those taken or left are the saved – only that a division will take place and that some will be ready for it and others not.

The need to be ready is emphasized by the shocking image of Christ's coming like a thief in the night. If the owner of a house had known when the thief was coming, he would know when to watch his goods and could safely neglect watching at all other times. But precisely because he does not know the time, even in general terms, his only safeguard is to be ready at all times. Just so, the Christian is called to await the Son of Man who "is coming at an unexpected hour".

Second Sunday of Advent

The Baptist Echoes the Prophet Isaiah

* 1st reading: Isaiah 11.1-10
* Psalm: 72
* 2nd reading: Romans 15.4-9
* Gospel: Matthew 3.1-12

In Advent, the Church hears proclaimed the message of Isaiah and, on the second and third Sundays, John the Baptist's call to repentance. In his preaching, the Baptist echoed Isaiah's message and showed its significance for a new era of salvation history.

The Book of Isaiah has been likened to an oratorio in which Israel sings its song of faith. The Isaian collection narrates the encounter of God's people with a series of imperial powers: the Assyrian, Babylonian and Persian empires. But this collection of visions cannot be classed either as mere political theory or history. Instead, its wonderful artistry holds the events of world history tightly bound within the purview of God's sovereignty.

In the prophetic view of Isaiah, decisions taken by Judean kings, their priestly advisors and imperial overlords are always penultimate. For the last word belongs to God, who clings to wonderful designs for Jerusalem. The "holy city" chosen by God is reckoned as the epitome of God's creation. In its suffering and destiny, it symbolizes the best hopes of the world for *shalom*: peace and well-being.

Jerusalem often struggled to have a life of its own without taking God into account. But God would have none of this. And so, Jerusalem underwent a series of chastisements for sin in order that, in the end, God might render the chastened city "healed, restored, ransomed, forgiven" (cf. Isaiah 65.18-19).

The closing words of chapter 10 spoke of God shaking "his fist at the mount of daughter Zion, the hill of Jerusalem" and hacking "down the thickets of the forest with an axe" (Isaiah 10.32, 34). Yet out of this sorry state of judgment, God foretold an utterly new beginning (found in chapter 11).

From the devastation of Jerusalem – the tree lopped off and cut down to size – God offered hope springing "from the stump of Jesse", the father of King David. A new kingly figure "shall grow out of his roots"; he will be a leader upon whom "the spirit of the Lord shall rest".

Endowed with the gifts of God's Spirit – wisdom and understanding, counsel and might, knowledge and the fear of the Lord – the coming one would enact all that is best in royal power ("with righteousness he shall judge the poor, and decide with equity for the meek of the earth").

This new era would bode well for the cosmic order because – in biblical perspective – disorders in human relationships are seen to spill over into disorders in creation. Conversely, reconciliation among human beings heralds not only restoration in nature but even an idyllic order of existence ("the wolf shall live with the lamb … the nursing child shall play over the hole of the asp"). In this perspective, renewed Jerusalem becomes a beacon to the world, because "they will not hurt or destroy on all my holy mountain".

Paul's remark in Romans that "whatever was written in former days was written for our instruction" expresses the believer's conviction that the prophecies of Isaiah present an ongoing challenge to the faith communities of Israel and the Church, as·well as an offer "that by steadfastness and by the encouragement of the Scriptures we might have hope".

In Matthew's Gospel, John the Baptist appears suddenly and abruptly, much as God's interventions do in salvation history. Elijah, whose garb and way of life the Baptist evoked, startled Israel with a radical call to faith. So, too, did John, whose message – "Repent, for the kingdom of heaven has come near" – parallels word-for-word the message of Jesus (cf. 4.17).

Christian tradition saw in John the Baptist not only Elijah come back to renew God's people, but the one Isaiah foretold as "the voice of one crying out in the wilderness: 'Prepare the way of the Lord, make his paths straight'". As Isaiah had foretold the humbling of God's people through the lopping off of trees grown too tall, so did the Baptist declare that "the axe is lying at the root of the trees".

However, this word of judgment is only part of God's design. The positive dimension is that God is continually at work, renewing a repentant people sincerely "confessing their sins". Attested by God, Jesus continues through his Church to proclaim good news and to baptize the contrite "with the Holy Spirit and fire".

Third Sunday of Advent

John the Baptist Wonders About Jesus

* 1st reading: Isaiah 35.1-6a, 10
* Psalm: 146
* 2nd reading: James 5.7-10
* Gospel: Matthew 11.2-11

n the closing words of last Sunday's gospel, John the Baptist foretold the career of the more powerful one "coming after me" who would baptize them "with the Holy Spirit and fire". This end-time figure would complete the Baptizer's mission of the judgment and renewal of God's people: "His winnowing fork is in his hand, and he will clear his threshing floor and will gather his wheat into the granary; but the chaff he will burn with unquenchable fire".

But Jesus' ministry was anything but a visitation of fire and judgment. Rather, he showed compassion, even to upsetting people's expectations by eating with sinners. Jesus carried out his mandate as God's anointed by powerful preaching and, surprisingly, a healing and miracle-working service.

So today's gospel passage depicts John the Baptist expressing wonder about Jesus when, from prison, he sent emissaries to Jesus asking, "Are you the one who is to come, or are we to wait for another?"

Many Church Fathers found it difficult to accept these words at face value. They were convinced that John made this inquiry for the sake of his disciples. Others felt that John spoke in this way to lure Jesus into making a public declaration or claimed that the Baptist did not doubt Jesus' identity, but only his way of presenting himself. Tertullian was an exception to the other early interpreters; he believed that John's doubts were genuine because the Spirit had been taken from him.

Whatever one's conclusions about the wonder of John, Jesus' reply to John drew attention to the marvellous happenings of Jesus' ministry, to "what you see and hear": the blind see, the lame walk, lepers are healed, the deaf are raised "and the poor have good news brought to them". Jesus' declaration echoes the language of several passages of Isaiah (cf. 26.19; 29.18-19; 35.5-10; 42.7, 18; 61.1-2).

Jesus' answer to the Baptist also summarizes all that Jesus has done since the beginning of his ministry (Matthew 4–10). Jesus implies that he is the "Coming One" heralded by John, the Messiah of Israelite prophecy, who brings to fulfillment the messianic oracles that Isaish uttered long ago by his proclamation to the poor and by miraculous and compassionate deeds.

ARCHBISHOP TERRENCE PRENDERGAST

Jesus' final words to John were a blessing that included an invitation to faith: "blessed is anyone who takes no offence at me". Why John or anyone else might be "scandalized" – that is, take offence and so fail to believe – is not spelled out, but must be related to the discrepancy between popular expectations about how the Messiah would carry out his functions and what people observed in Jesus.

If the Coming One was to usher in the end times, people might have been asking themselves, "Where is the judgment that should accompany this stage in salvation history?" This is an issue that Jesus studiously avoided in his citation of Isaiah. In effect, Jesus was saying that judgment comes later and that other things come first.

Scholars have seen in Jesus' use of the *beatitude* form ("blessed is the one/ blessed are they...") here and elsewhere (cf. Matthew 5.3-6; 13.16-17) evidence of his messianic consciousness. You see, recognition of Jesus makes one truly blessed.

Though the closing words of today's gospel passage relativize his greatness ("among those born of women no one has arisen greater than John the Baptist; yet the least in the kingdom of heaven is greater than he"), Jesus praises John as a prophet who carried out an important mission in difficult circumstances.

The Jordan River valley contained reeds blowing in the wind. Since Herod had built palaces out there (the ruins of Herodion, Machaerus and Masada are still impressive today), there were people out in the wilderness "dressed in soft robes".

Still, people yearning for repentance did not go out to see these, but to hear and heed the words of a powerful religious figure who came in the spirit of the prophet Elijah (cf. Matthew 11.13).

John played a decisive role in salvation history, preparing the eschatological events that came true in Jesus. Indeed, Jesus observed that John was also the object of prophecy, citing a combined reference to Exodus 23.20 and Malachi 3.1 ("See, I am sending my messenger ahead of you, who will prepare your way before you").

In the end, however, what matters most is not personal greatness, but belonging to the new era of God's reign inaugurated by Jesus.

God's Mysterious Coming in the Flesh

* 1st reading: Isaiah 7.10-14
* Psalm: 24
* 2nd reading: Romans 1.1-7
* Gospel: Matthew 1.18-24

In the ancient world, the standard opening of a letter was rather simple, much like our epistolary practice ("Dear Mary"): "Gaius to Claudia, greetings".

In Paul's early letters (e.g., First Thessalonians) he follows this simple form. But as his career matured, the description of himself and his recipients became increasingly complex.

The Letter to the Romans, which epitomizes the themes of Paul's gospel, is the most developed. In effect, all of today's second reading constitutes Paul's opening salutation to the church at Rome, one that – in contrast to the situation of his other letters – he had not founded.

This opening greeting culminates with Paul's deepest wish for all believers. "Grace to you and peace from God our Father and the Lord Jesus Christ".

After describing himself as a "servant" of Jesus Christ, Paul went on to note that he had been "called to be an Apostle, set apart for the gospel of God".

The purpose of this election by God is "the obedience of faith", a theme evoking Israel's vocation to be an obedient nation responsible for witnessing to God among the world's nations. Paul says that "the gospel concerning [God's] Son" has now made it possible for these nations of the world ("all the Gentiles") to leave the path of disobedience they had been following and, instead, to glorify God with their whole being.

The content of the gospel speaks about the messianic career of Jesus in two stages. We shall take these in reverse order:

"By resurrection from the dead" and through his entrance into the new era marked by the Spirit, the messianic candidate Jesus has been installed as Messiah in fact. God has inaugurated this new end-time age of liberation by declaring Jesus "to be Son of God with power according to the spirit of holiness". In other words, in Jesus' resurrection from the dead we see God's vindication of Jesus as his Son, a truth that was not always clear when people examined Jesus' earthly origins.

With regard to Jesus' earthly origins ("descended from David according to the flesh"), Paul says very little, except to convey the conviction he shared with early Christianity and some Jewish circles that Jesus had fulfilled a key requirement, namely birth of the royal house of David.

Today's gospel explores the early Church's reflection on the birth of Jesus in light of the Scriptures, notably today's first reading from Isaiah. "All this took place to fulfill what had been spoken by the Lord through the prophet: 'Look, the young woman is with child and shall bear a son, and shall name him *Emmanuel*".

In the perspective of Easter, the early Church, after reflecting on the Sacred Scriptures, could assert that Jesus had borne the name given him by the angel of the Lord, and that he had fulfilled God's purpose that he would "save his people from their sins". What is more, Jesus had been a *Davidid* – that is, a legal son and descendant of a true Davidid, Joseph – according to God's promise through Isaiah to the house of David.

Through his foster-father Joseph, Jesus was the Son of David. We should realize that Davidic sonship was a legal sonship that did not demand a biological relationship. Joseph knew that he had not fathered Mary's child. And he was prepared as "a righteous man" to fulfill the law's requirements towards his fiancée (he "planned to dismiss her quietly").

What the religious law required was that his mother's husband acknowledge Jesus as his own. This Joseph did when, after being informed of God's intent in a dream, he chose to remain with Mary and to give Jesus his name.

Since Jesus had been conceived by his mother Mary of the Holy Spirit ("she was found to be with child from the Holy Spirit"), Jesus' mysterious origin lay fundamentally with God. Jesus' divine Sonship came about in a different way. Jesus had a biological mother but no human, biological father.

The gospel's message is both simple and profound, told with enthusiasm yet restraint. A righteous man receives a revelation to which he is submissive and obedient. Joseph manifested the "obedience of faith" that Paul speaks about and, in this way, is a model for every believer.

Feast of Christmas – December 25

Light Shining in the Darkness

* 1st reading: Isaiah 9.2-7
* Psalm: 96
* 2nd reading: Titus 2.11-14
* Gospel: Luke 2.1-16

Among the customs of Christmas is the lighting of a Christmas candle. People place it in the windows of their homes, at the centre of their living rooms or on dining room tables. Some say the candle is to welcome Christ, should he favour them with a visit. Not for them the shame of turning away the Saviour, as happened in Bethlehem two thousand years ago. Their aim is to show hospitality to the Light of the World, in whatever way he chooses to come to them.

There may be some fancy in the way the meaning of the Christmas candle is explained or enacted in various homes. At its core, however, this custom tries to embody the heart of the Christian gospel. God, who was revealed in Jesus' birth in poverty and obscurity

ARCHBISHOP TERRENCE PRENDERGAST

centuries ago, comes into the world with the purpose of drawing near to the people he greatly loves.

As a symbol, the candle is one that – by its light – invites, while also promising a welcome. As it burns, the candle offers warmth against the cold, light in the face of winter's darkness, and the comfort of friendship and family to those who experience neither in the chill of our modern, technological society.

The prophet Isaiah uses several images to express the dynamics of God's coming among his people. To appreciate the radiant light and hope that Isaiah foresees, we must contrast it with the gloomy darkness he mentioned in the passage just before today's first reading: "[People] will turn their faces upward", Isaiah says," or they will look to the earth, but will see only distress and darkness, the gloom of anguish; and they will be thrust into thick darkness" (Isaiah 8.21-22). This is the extremity of God-forsakenness from which the light of the Prince of Peace rescues his fellow humans!

Only when the human condition has sunk to its utter depths of darkness and despair can one see that God's intervention brings light. And with light comes hope. "The people who walked in darkness have seen a great light; those who lived in a land of deep darkness – on them light has shone."

God's light brings with it joy. But not an ephemeral or shallow joy. Rather, a joy like that experienced in the relief, peace and sense of accomplishment that follows the bringing in of a harvest. Or what war-weary people feel at the cessation of hostilities.

The spiritual vitality experienced is like that which surfaces in a soul when a burden is lifted from a person's shoulders. Or the joy one feels when the rod of an oppressor is finally shattered. Truly, it is a light by whose glow a whole new social order can be imagined! "There shall be endless peace ... with justice and with righteousness from this time onward and forevermore."

Christians also see the candle's light as representing not only their readiness to receive Jesus, but also Christ's readiness to give himself. Disciples discover in the birth of the Lord Jesus that light – unique beyond all others – that has truly enlightened the world. "Then an

Angel of the Lord stood before [the shepherds] and the glory of the Lord shone round them.... And suddenly there was with the Angel a multitude of the heavenly host, praising God and saying, 'Glory to God in the highest heaven, and on earth peace among those whom he favours!'"

Christ casts his glow on all – ourselves included – who, to one degree or another, sit in the deep darkness Isaiah spoke about.

Christ Jesus does this to share with us every good thing that belongs to the Father's kingdom, especially the peace and joy that God alone can give. If men, women and children let it, such a gift from God can transform them.

As Paul remarks to Titus, by Christ's incarnation God purified his people, making them a "people of his own who are zealous for good deeds."

Knowing this deep truth of Christmas, we are truly blessed. In confident hope, we can draw near to Christ, the Light of the World. We do so with that same ease and peace with which we draw near to the Christmas candle.

The Holy Family of Jesus, Mary and Joseph

Christian Family Life: Adaptable and Holy

* 1st reading: Sirach 3.2-6, 12-14
* Psalm: 128
* 2nd reading: Colossians 3.12-21
* Gospel: Matthew 2.13-15, 19-23

The challenges to family life that believers face in changing times are not new. The ancient commandment "Honour your father and your mother" held a promise: "so that your days may be long in the land that the Lord your God is giving you" (Exodus 20.12; cf. Deuteronomy 5.16).

ARCHBISHOP TERRENCE PRENDERGAST

Israel's stress on the reverence to be shown one's parents reflected a sociological context in which adult sons continued to live within the family unit long after they married. The fourth commandment, then, applied not only to youngsters at home but to adults living with aging parents.

The sage Ben Sira, writing between 200 and 180 BC, extended the implications of the commandment by urging his readers to continue to respect their parents, even when senility placed strains on family relations ("help your parents in your old age..., even if their minds fail, be patient with them").

The extended family's tendency to live in close quarters must have put an enormous burden on younger family members when their elderly parents began to lack judgment. Kindness in such circumstances would bear rich dividends and atone for earlier faults ("kindness to your father will not be forgotten, and will be credited to you against your sins"). True religion moves from the idealized realm and faces the challenge of parents in declining years when they may become difficult and excessively demanding.

Paul's letter to the Colossians straddled the meaning of salvation in Christ for the cosmos and the nitty-gritty world where most people lived their lives: wives and husbands, children and parents, slaves and masters.

As a result of their baptism into Christ, the Christians of Colossae were addressed with the privileged titles shared by Israel in the past: "God's chosen ones, holy and beloved". Paul urged them to dress themselves with virtues attributed to God and to Christ, "compassion, kindness, humility, meekness, and patience".

An important accessory that complements the fully-dressed Christian is love ("clothe yourselves with love, which binds everything together in perfect harmony").

Christ's peace is to govern every aspect of the readers' lives as they relate to one another in a changing Hellenistic culture. Christ, the Lord of peace, is to rule kindly in their midst. The word of Christ – the gospel message that centres on Christ – ought to lead the Colossians to mutually teach and admonish each other in a helpful and tactful way.

The final exhortation, before particular instructions are given, is universal in scope, covering every aspect of life: "Whatever you do, in word or deed, do everything in the name of the Lord Jesus, giving thanks to God the Father through him".

The closing verses of the second reading – with instructions for slaves and masters omitted – constitute what is known as a *household code*: guidelines for good living offered to each member of the household unit. These are found in several other later New Testament letters (cf. Ephesians 5.21–6.9; 1 Peter 2.18–3.7; Titus 2.1-10; 1 Timothy 2.8-15; 6.1-2).

Scholars, preachers and ordinary Christians are divided on the pertinence of this teaching. Even the lectionary notes that a shorter reading may end just before the injunction "Wives, be subject to your husbands", with which the household code begins. But there is a rich teaching on mutual love that one may note above and beyond superficial first impressions of what is said in the text.

In each case, the subordinate members in the Hellenistic social setting (wives, children, slaves) are addressed first. But they are treated as ethically responsible partners who are called to act "as is fitting in the Lord".

For their part, husbands are to show unceasing care for their wives' total well-being. Though no motivation for the husband's devotion to his wife is given in Colossians, a lengthy text paralleling the husband's love for his wife with Christ's self-sacrificing love for the Church is found in Ephesians 5.25-33.

Christian children are to obey their parents, "for this is your acceptable duty in the Lord". Though young, they are old enough to know that their relationship to Jesus affects their behaviour at home.

Parents, especially fathers, are not to irritate or provoke their children, lest they become discouraged. There should be firm guidance but no discouragement in today's adaptable and adapting family striving to be holy.

ARCHBISHOP TERRENCE PRENDERGAST

The Solemnity of Mary,
the Holy Mother of God – January 1

Mary "Pondered in Her Heart"

* 1st reading: Numbers 6.22-27
* Psalm: 67
* 2nd reading: Galatians 4.4-7
* Gospel: Luke 2.16-21

At Christmas, the Scripture readings focused on the Lord Jesus come into the world to save humanity. Today's liturgy emphasizes the effect Jesus' presence had on the shepherds and in the life of Mary. Her struggle to understand what God was accomplishing in her life serves as a model for all who are called to believe the good news of God's active presence in their lives.

A little-known book, Numbers presents God's people Israel as a faith community on the march. Aaron's blessing climaxes two chapters that describe the role of priests in the faith community. Through their privileges and responsibilities, priests safeguarded the people's purity as God's holy people and called down divine blessings.

The blessing of Aaron has a three-fold structure, offering God's people security, prosperity and well-being ("the Lord bless you and keep you; the Lord make his face to shine upon you … and give you peace"). The prayer formula is in the second person singular, suggesting that God blesses the community through care of each individual.

Only in the light of Easter could the Church fully grasp the unique role of Jesus as Lord, Christ and Saviour. However, the truths that the Church would understand clearly only after Jesus' death and resurrection, the evangelists have anticipated in their description of the events they relate in the infancy narratives, which are called cameos of the gospel message.

A similar development may be discerned in the Church's understanding of the role in God's saving plan of Jesus' mother, Mary. Luke preserves traditions concerning Mary, including her presence at the birth of the Church at Pentecost (Acts 1.14–2.42).

The Holy Spirit, poured out in fullness on Mary that day, brought to mature expression her pondering upon the events surrounding Jesus' conception and birth, and his manifestation to the shepherds and to others.

In today's gospel, Luke gives hints of who Mary would become – the disciple come to full faith in her son, Jesus, as Messiah and Saviour. For what she ultimately became was present implicitly in her receptivity to God's action in her son's conception and birth, in the shepherds' proclamation and in the other events of the infancy gospel.

The shepherds told everyone in the house that what had been announced to them about the Child Jesus had come true. When God acts – as he had done in Jesus' birth – amazement is the usual human reaction in the Bible. Among those who "were amazed" was Mary. But her response, unlike that of others, was singled out for special mention: "Mary treasured all these words and pondered them in her heart."

Luke did not specify the precise nature of Mary's pondering. It seems we are to understand that she juxtaposed – in her inner being – the shepherds' visit along with what had already happened in her life.

In this pondering, Mary was not a passive observer. Rather, she inwardly and actively sought to understand more fully what God had been revealing in these events, and why it was that, in God's design, she should have a role in these extraordinary happenings. Each Christian faces a similar challenge – to sort out, in our own life, the wonders the Lord is doing in our life.

In writing to the Galatians, Paul reflected on God's Son having been "born of a woman, born under the law." The first phrase stresses Jesus' true humanity, implying his ability to represent all humanity. The second phrase emphasizes that Jesus came into this world as a

Jew to fulfill the Torah. In doing so, Jesus revealed its purpose and enabled all who are guided by the Spirit to live now as children of God.

Paul said that all believers, through their share in the gift of the Spirit in baptism, can cry out to God with Jesus' exclamation, "Abba! Father!" In Paul's view, what Jesus was by nature – God's Son, God's Child – Christians have become by adoption.

The message of their adoption as God's children is something Christians delight in discovering again and again. With the power of divine adoption working in their lives, Christians experience – as Mary did in her active pondering – "the freedom of the glory of the children of God" (cf. Romans 8.21).

Epiphany of the Lord –
Sunday between January 2 and 8

The Radiant Glory of the Lord

* 1st reading: Isaiah 60.1-6
* Psalm: 72
* 2nd reading: Ephesians 3.2-3a, 5-6
* Gospel: Matthew 2.1-12

Towards the end of a sabbatical in the Holy Land, I was privileged to preside at the Eucharist on Pentecost. Our group included representatives of several linguistic backgrounds (Arabic, English, French, German, Polish, Spanish), and we used all of these languages in the readings and prayers.

A unity in faith, forged among us during our year together, came to a prayerful expression at Mass. This unity reflected the message of Ephesians: "the Gentiles have become fellow heirs, members of the same body, and sharers in the promise in Christ Jesus through the gospel".

Our celebration was held on Mount Nebo, site of the death of Moses. There a modernistic sculpture dominates the courtyard of the church: the bronze serpent pinned to a cross, which brought healing to God's people in the wilderness (Numbers 21.9) and fore-shadowed the salvation God offers the world in Christ crucified (John 3.14-16). The mystery of God's design for the healing of the world, though hidden from humanity, Paul says, has been revealed "to his holy apostles and prophets by the Spirit".

That evening we looked out over the Jordan Rift and could see the night lights of Amman and Jerusalem. From one angle, these cities are close to one another; yet from another, until recently, they could have been on different planets, so hostile were the relations between Israel and Jordan. Halting steps towards reconciliation have begun many times, with mostly tragic results. Still, a great healing process is needed before Jerusalem truly becomes the city of peace and justice foretold as her destiny.

Isaiah imagined Jerusalem possessing radiance more glorious than the modern city aglitter with artificial light. With a double impera-tive, "Arise, shine!" the prophet urges the inhabitants of Jerusalem, after their return from exile, to see God radiating a dazzling pres-ence from within the city. The prophet imagined that the darkness of the past would surrender to the light and that nations would be drawn to the Holy City by the magnetic attraction of its wealth and beauty ("your heart shall thrill and rejoice, because the abundance of the sea shall be brought to you, the wealth of the nations shall come to you").

The names "Midian, Ephah, Sheba" in the closing verses of Isaiah and "Tarshish, Sheba and Seba" in the psalm refer to desert dwellers of the Arabian Peninsula and inhabitants of islands in the Mediterranean. An immense worldwide empire is envisioned, with all coming under the authority of the Davidic king, a notion implied in the Magi offering homage to the newborn king.

The Magi were a caste of wise men that interpreters have associ-ated with astrology, magic, Zoroastrianism or the interpretation of dreams. In times of social upheaval and massive change, like that of Jesus or our own days, people are drawn to astral religion because the stars offer regularity and order.

ARCHBISHOP TERRENCE PRENDERGAST

Problematically, however, such religious observances make people feel helpless, subject to impersonal fate. In the gospel, the star serves God's purpose and leads the Magi to Jesus, to whose rule they surrender themselves.

The true guide to God's purpose in the world may be found not in the stars but in the Sacred Scriptures. When the Magi arrived in Jerusalem, they inquired where they might find "the child who has been born king of the Jews". Herod the Great, who was so paranoid in his later years that he killed his favourite wife and two of his sons, interpreted this question as an inquiry about 'the Messiah'.

Consultations with the religious leaders about the evidence of Scripture pointed to Bethlehem. Two texts have been combined as a testimony to this truth: "And you, Bethlehem, in the land of Judah, are by no means least among the rulers of Judah (Micah 5.2); for from you shall come a ruler who is to shepherd my people Israel" (2 Samuel 5.2).

Neither the religious leaders nor Herod seemed interested in acting on the Scriptures. But the Magi did. They found great joy in the reappearance of the star and in discovering the Christ Child, to whom they gave precious gifts. The Scriptures guide us to Christ; surrendering to him requires a personal decision. But yielding to the message about Christ, as the Magi did, helps transform our local Jerusalems into places of justice and peace.

The Baptism of the Lord

"To Fulfill All Righteousness"

* 1st reading: Isaiah 42.1-4, 6-7
* Psalm: 29
* 2nd reading: Acts 10.34-38
* Gospel: Matthew 3.13-17

One of the major features of Matthew's account of Jesus' baptism by John the Baptist is their conversation before the water ritual was enacted. Matthew's account also suggests that the crowd did not witness the accompanying supernatural events. If that is the case, then what occurred at the time of the baptism – rather than the baptism itself – appears to centre the reader's attention.

For many in the early Church, there was a problematic aspect in Jesus' having been baptized by John: namely, the implication that Jesus needed to repent. Among the synoptic accounts (the Gospels of Matthew, Mark and Luke), only Matthew's narrative addresses this issue, while at the same time treating the continuity and discontinuity between the Baptist and Jesus.

Matthew's opening words point to Jesus' intention in leaving Galilee and coming to the Jordan. Purposefully, Matthew notes, Jesus approached John "to be baptized by him". In other words, Jesus had already decided when he was in Nazareth to undergo baptism.

Jesus was determined and would not be dissuaded by John's protest, "I need to be baptized by you, and do you come to me?" John recognized Jesus as his superior and tried to reverse the action that was about to take place. At that point, Jesus spoke for the first time in the gospel narrative and took charge of his own baptism.

Jesus' reply, which states that he wished to submit to John's baptism ("Let it be so now; for it is proper for us in this way to fulfill all righteousness"), introduces us to two key emphases of the Matthean gospel: "fulfillment" and "righteousness".

In the Sermon on the Mount, "righteousness" is the main goal of a disciple's following of Jesus (cf. 5.20; 6.1, 33). Fundamentally, then, fulfilling all righteousness means accomplishing God's will in all its fullness.

Why did Jesus need to be baptized by John? Throughout the ages, saints and scholars have struggled to answer this question.

Not because he was a sinner, though some commentators today suggest this answer. Nor was it only to identify with the Baptist's movement, though God's appeal had gone out to all Israel through John and Jesus saw answering his summons as a religious duty.

More correctly, as some claim, by his baptism Jesus showed his solidarity with sinful people in their need. As a representative figure, the Messiah – like the Servant of the Lord that Isaiah spoke of – was the embodiment of Israel.

Identifying fully with God's people, Jesus obediently acted out his role and received the Spirit's anointing to fully carry out his mission. This mission set Jesus on the path that would ultimately lead to his death on the cross, the fullest measure of his identification with sinful humanity.

As the agent of God who would bring the kingdom to its full visible manifestation, Jesus symbolized strength and authority befitting the Son of God and Son of David.

Yet, Jesus also appears in Matthew's gospel as one who is humble and obedient, thus fulfilling the description of God's (suffering) servant foretold by Isaiah: "He will not cry or lift up his voice, or make it heard in the street; a bruised reed he will not break, and a dimly burning wick he will not quench" (cf. Matthew 12.18-21).

The other divine actors in the drama are suggested by the heavens being torn open (by God the Father) and the presence of the "Spirit of God descending like a dove and alighting on him".

In interpreting the symbolism of the dove, several meanings have been offered; the more plausible ones include the beginning of a new creation in Jesus or the end of the age of judgment (proclaimed by John).

While Mark and Luke depict the voice from heaven as directed to Jesus ("you are my Son" [cf. Mark 1.11; Luke 3.22]), for Matthew the Father's testimony is objective ("This is my Son, the Beloved, with whom I am well pleased").

God's voice, speaking directly from heaven, with authority, serves the Church as a catechetical and confessional formula. In a similar vein, Peter's speech in Acts declares the Church's conviction that at his baptism "God anointed Jesus of Nazareth with the Holy Spirit and with power; ... he went about doing good and healing all who were oppressed by the devil, for God was with him".

Second Sunday in Ordinary Time

Jesus Is the One Who Baptizes with the Holy Spirit

* 1st reading: Isaiah 49.3, 5-6
* Psalm: 27
* 2nd reading: 1 Corinthians 1.1-3
* Gospel: John 1.29-34

Allusions to Jesus' baptism by John in today's gospel afford Christian disciples an opportunity to reflect on this mystery in our Lord's life, and on the implications for their lives of the baptism in the Holy Spirit that Jesus has conferred on them.

Following its majestic Prologue ("In the beginning was the Word" [John 1.1-18]), the first chapter of John's gospel passes on to the Baptist's testimony to Jesus and the coming of disciples to him (1.19-51). A crescendo of titles leads the reader to discover Jesus' identity as the "Lamb of God" (1.29), "God's Chosen One" (the likely variant for "the Son of God" in 1.34), "Rabbi" (= "Teacher" 1.38), "Messiah/Christ" (1.41), "Son of God" (1.49), "King of Israel" (1.49), and "Son of Man" (1.51).

Some have suggested that John's testimony, especially his description of Jesus as "the Lamb of God who takes away the sin of the world", cannot have a historical foundation, as this would presuppose a post-Easter understanding of Jesus' death that the Baptist could not have had. Yet, it is possible that John imagined Jesus as the warrior lamb of apocalyptic literature who would blot out the world's sin by a terrifying and powerful act of judgment. Instead, Jesus offered himself as an expiatory sacrifice on the cross, taking away sin by absorbing all the evil of the world in his broken body.

The irony of John's confession is a typical feature of the Fourth Evangelist's narrative. Later in the gospel, when Caiaphas speaks of the necessity that "one man die for the people", the evangelist points

ARCHBISHOP TERRENCE PRENDERGAST

out how right the high priest was, foretelling that Jesus would gather into one the scattered people of God (11.49-52). This confession also exposes the reader to the divine pedagogy whereby those who are open to the life of faith are gradually led to understand how Jesus meets human hopes and fulfills divine promises.

Though Jesus appeared on the stage of history after John the Baptist, we learn that Jesus outstrips John by reason of Jesus' pre-existence ("After me comes a man who ranks ahead of me because he was before me"). John's baptizing with water had only one goal: that Jesus "might be revealed to Israel". In his turn, Jesus transformed the very nature of the rite of baptism, for he is "the one who baptizes with the Holy Spirit". Jesus is able to baptize in this way because, at his baptism, the Holy Spirit descended and remained on him. Elsewhere, we learn that God "gives the Spirit without measure" (3.34) to Jesus.

As the bearer and giver of the Spirit, Jesus communicates the salvation won by his death on the cross to all who yearn for it. In John's gospel, those who hunger and thirst for God are invited to live by faith and become, through their encounter with Jesus, God's chosen ones ("those who are sanctified in Christ Jesus, called to be saints"). For Jesus, who calls disciples into fellowship with him and one another, does so as God's Chosen One *par excellence*, the suffering servant of the Lord.

Today's first reading is from one of four passages in Deutero-Isaiah known as the Servant Poems (42.1-7; 49.1-7; 50.4-9; 52.13–53.12). These poetic pieces are striking additions to their contexts. They speak of God's Servant having been entrusted with a silent mission to the people Israel and the nations of the world. Disciplined by suffering, the Servant – though humiliated and abused – is commissioned anew ("to raise up the tribes of Jacob ... that my salvation may reach to the end of the earth").

Interpretations of the Servant have oscillated between a collective view (Israel) and an individual of great holiness (the Messiah). Christians applied this messianic interpretation to Jesus, convinced that Jesus so identified himself. These ideas may be combined by seeing that, through the sacrament of baptism, Jesus shares his personal mission with his disciples. As God's servants in the One Servant, Christians should delight to carry out their baptismal service with the same disposition as Jesus, making the Psalmist's sentiment their own: "Here I am ... I delight to do your will, O my God; your law is within my heart".

Third Sunday in Ordinary Time

"Repent: Be United in the Same Mind"

* 1st reading: Isaiah 9.1-4
* Psalm: 27
* 2nd reading: 1 Corinthians 1.10-13, 17-18
* Gospel: Matthew 4.12-23

Zebulun, Naphtali and the Coastal Highway on the west side of the Jordan River, a region known as "Galilee of the Gentiles", had been humiliated by the Assyrian king Tiglath-Pileser III in 733 BC (2 Kings 15.29). In place of this lowly state, God pledged glorification.

Humiliation-glorification is only one of several pairs of contrasts intertwined within Isaiah's prophetic word. Darkness will give way to light, sadness to joy and oppression to victory.

Harvest time and the sharing of the spoils are periods of celebration. The work that went into cultivating the crop has borne fruit. The sacrifices and discipline of battle have won the victory. People deserve to relax and enjoy the peace and plenty that have come.

In salvation history, the victory of Gideon against Midian (Judges 7.15-25) featured a small contingent battling against mighty forces. Their triumph, with soldiers from Naphtali, had become proverbial of what Israel could do with God's blessing. It became a symbol of the victory Jesus won through his proclamation of the kingdom and gathering the nucleus of his future Church.

ARCHBISHOP TERRENCE PRENDERGAST

Early Christians saw in Jesus the fulfillment of Isaiah's prophecy concerning Zebulun and Napthali ("the people who walked in darkness have seen a great light; those who lived in the land of deep darkness – on them a light has shined"). For Jesus embodies their light, their joy and their victory – not as the leader of warring armies triumphing over Israel's enemies, but by his simple gesture, as a working man, of settling down in a Galilean city and beginning to proclaim good news from God.

Matthew's early gospel chapters show how what Jesus did – even choosing Capernaum in Galilee as the base for his ministry – fulfilled Old Testament hopes. Jesus' message "Repent, for the kingdom of heaven has come near" paralleled, word for word, John the Baptist's summons (cf. Matthew 3.2). The evangelist says thereby that there is a consistency in God's message through the ages into the era of the Church.

Yet, even with this divine consistency in God's appeal for reformed lives that accept the kingdom, there was something utterly new in Jesus' approach. This appears in the dynamic way he drew followers to leave possessions and trades (Simon and Andrew leave their boats and fishing tackle) and even family (the sons of Zebedee leave their father). These disciples entered onto the path of the kingdom.

In those days, young people sought out a rabbi to learn from him the ways of God. Instead, Jesus – more than a rabbi, though he is a teacher – takes the initiative in calling followers for the kingdom.

Throughout his gospel, Matthew illustrates his conviction that Jesus is a leader powerful in word and deed. Also, Jesus' deeds are fully consistent with the message he speaks – a value he holds out to every man, woman or child who wishes to be his disciple.

Matthew communicates this truth by means of a summary description of Jesus' activity, which Matthew uses twice to frame the early stages of Jesus' career (Matthew 4.23; 9.35). The healings and cures are a visible expression in people's lives of God's gift to them of the kingdom through the preaching of Jesus, a proclamation continued today by and in the Church of Jesus Christ.

Despite our tendency to idealize the early Church, Paul's letters to the Corinthians show that divisions and rivalries were present almost from the beginning.

As one reads through First Corinthians, we find people who see themselves as strong and others weak. Some claim to be "in the know" while others are not. Some are "ascetics" and others are "libertines" in the area of sexual ethics. While all proclaimed that Jesus Christ was risen from the dead, Paul felt some denied that truth by the way they lived.

Paul makes an appeal to unity today that repeats Jesus' gospel call to repent. Paul tries to get people to see ("by the name of our Lord Jesus Christ") that it is unity, not division, that Christ wishes among his followers. It is an apt message in this period of the Week of Prayer for Christian Unity. For, even in today's Church, Catholic Christians need to "be united in the same mind and the same purpose", rather than being partisans of one or another viewpoint within the Church.

Fourth Sunday in Ordinary Time

The Charter Principles of God's Kingdom

* 1st reading: Zephaniah 2.3, 3.12-13
* Psalm: 146
* 2nd reading: 1 Corinthians 1.26-31
* Gospel: Matthew 5.1-12

While visiting the families of several of my priests, I had occasion in the late 1990s to travel in Poland, a society in transition. All observers agreed that it was one of the countries that was succeeding in the transition from Communist control to a market economy. The journals travellers receive were telling how the energies of the nation were preparing for the country's entry

ARCHBISHOP TERRENCE PRENDERGAST

into the European Economic Community early in the third millennium. Poland, they said, was prepared to pay the price involved in
economic restructuring to make this happen smoothly.

But there was a darker side to the changes: a great deal of un-
employment, migration from rural areas to the cities, and social
disruptions symbolized by drugs, prostitution, a criminal underworld,
social anxiety.

Still, the people continued in large numbers to attend Sunday
Mass, value confession and make pilgrimages to Our Lady of
Czestochowa, to the chapel of the Divine Mercy where Saint
Faustina lies buried, and to countless other shrines across the coun-
tryside. One wonders what role the Catholic faith – which continues
to unite families and the Polish nation – would play in the social
transformations lying ahead.

The prophet Zephaniah, too, lived in a difficult time of transi-
tions, during King Josiah's reign (around 640 BC), when the southern
kingdom of Judah existed in subjection as a vassal state of Assyria.
Pagan morality and idolatrous worship were beginning to make
incursions upon the faith of Israel.

Like the prophets Amos and Isaiah before him, Zephaniah pro-
tested against this diminishment of biblical religion. He foretold
that the blazing wrath of the Lord God would flare up against Israel
on the coming "day of the Lord" (1.8-18; 2.2).

Our passage opens with a triple appeal to seek out the Lord and
his values ("seek righteousness, seek humility"). Zephaniah was opposed to the empty formalism found in many religious practices, so
he did not imagine that people should seek God at some sanctuary.
Rather, God was to be discovered in obedience to the divine will, in
practising justice and in turning aside from haughtiness or pride.

What is striking is that, while much of this behaviour is clearly
human cooperation with God's directives, it is also – fundamentally
– God's doing ("For I will leave in the midst of you a people humble
and lowly"). This tiny remnant of God's creation shall seek their
refuge "in the name of the Lord ..., they shall do no wrong and utter
no lies, ... and no one shall make them afraid".

This insight – that the holy remnant of Israel is the product of God's initiative and human cooperation with God's plan – is an important principle for interpreting the Sermon on the Mount (chapters 5–7), the first of five great addresses Jesus gives in Matthew's gospel (the others are in chapters 10, 13, 18, 24 and 25).

For the Sermon, which lays out the charter principles of the kingdom of heaven, begins, in the first beatitude, with God's gift of the kingdom ("Blessed are the poor in spirit, for theirs is the kingdom of heaven"). God's gift then calls out for a response, as we shall see more fully in next week's gospel ("You are the light of the world ...; let your light shine before human beings, so that they may see your good works and give glory to your Father in heaven").

But the reciprocal process – of God giving and humans responding – is already found within the very dynamic movement of the eight beatitudes. Those who know their interior spiritual poverty through experiences such as mourning begin to hunger also for the things of God and for right relationships in this world. Jesus promises that God, who has prompted these desires and yearnings in the little ones whom he has blessed with the kingdom, will fulfill their every aspiration: "Blessed are those who hunger and thirst for righteousness, for they will be filled. Blessed are the peacemakers, for they will be called children of God".

God's paradoxical bestowal of blessings on the lowly is expressed also in Paul's writings. Before baptism, Paul says, few of the Corinthians were "wise by human standards; not many were powerful". So God chose "what is foolish in the world to shame the wise ... what is weak in the world to shame the strong". In other words, kingdom values become embodied in the lives of Jesus' followers.

ARCHBISHOP TERRENCE PRENDERGAST

Religious Ritual in Family Life

* 1st reading: Malachi 3.1-4
* Psalm: 24
* 2nd reading: Hebrews 2.10-11, 13b-18
* Gospel: Luke 2.22-40 or 2.22-32

During a journey to India, I visited the temple of the goddess Kali in Calcutta. There, families and individuals brought offerings of various kinds as part of their devotions. I watched as one family sacrificed a goat. Each person had a part to play in the service.

Various ritual gestures were carried out by the mother, father and children (touching the sacrificial stump, anointing themselves with blood, and so on). It was clear that this family had done these things many times before and that the rituals had been absorbed into their family and personal lives.

We see this same reality at work in the gospel story that we call "the presentation of the child Jesus in the Temple", the purification ritual following his birth. On the eighth day after his birth, Jesus was circumcised, a rite that marked in his flesh that he belonged to the covenant community that originated with God's promises to Abraham. At that time, too, Jesus formally received the name given him by the angel Gabriel.

Jewish ritual demanded two other gestures of devotion: the "buying back" from God of the firstborn and the purification of the mother. God asked families in subsequent generations to recall the Exodus by consecrating to him their firstborn child (Exodus 13.2, 11-16).

Later, the price of the redemption was set at five shekels (Numbers 18.15-16). In another development, the priestly service of the Levites was said to take the place of this offering and atonement (8.14-19).

Luke does not depict the Holy Family fulfilling this act of redemption. The reading from Hebrews describes Jesus as the source of atonement: "[Jesus] had to become like his brothers and sisters in every respect, so that he might be a merciful and faithful high priest in the service of God, to make a sacrifice of atonement for the sins of the people".

Following a male child's birth, the mother was ceremonially unclean for seven days and underwent purification for another 33 days; the period was twice as long for a female child (cf. Leviticus 12.1-5). At the end of the 40 (or 80) days, the Jewish mother was to offer a lamb, a pigeon and a turtledove. The poor could offer, instead, two turtledoves or pigeons (Leviticus 12.6-8). Luke's account describes the act as "their purification", which suggests he was unaware that the ritual applied only to the mother or that he viewed the entire ritual as a family matter.

It was while carrying out this ritual "according to the law of Moses" that the Holy Family encountered in the Temple at Jerusalem two other devout Jews: the prophets Simeon and Anna. Simeon is described as "righteous and devout", a person who longed for the "consolation of Israel". From Malachi we learn that some Israelites believed the messianic era would involve a dramatic divine intervention in the Temple. The prophet has God declaring that "the Lord whom you seek will suddenly come to his temple".

The Holy Spirit promised Simeon that he would see the Messiah before his death, and guided him to Jesus. So the Temple and the ritual activity in it become the occasion for a profound spiritual encounter. Simeon then faces his death with consolation and peace ("Master, now you are dismissing your servant in peace ...."). Simeon can meet death with serenity, for Jesus is the one who frees "those who all their lives were held in slavery by the fear of death".

Anna's ritual practices of devotion were likewise blessed ("She never left the temple but worshipped there with fasting and prayer night and day"). Having met Jesus, she could speak of the fulfillment of their desires to "all who were looking for the redemption of Jerusalem".

Luke described Jesus and his family as observant Jews on several occasions, such as their annual pilgrimage to Jerusalem for Passover, his regular Sabbath presence in the synagogue, and his frequent prayer (cf. Luke 2.41; 4.16; 6.12; 9.28).

This reality and today's gospel hint that Catholic ritual devotions (morning and evening prayers, Sunday Mass, Friday abstinence, Lenten fasting) serve to dispose those who practice them for encounters with the divine.

Christian families might want to keep this in mind particularly as the coming seasons of Lent and Easter offer opportunities to know the Lord Jesus better.

Fifth Sunday in Ordinary Time

Salt for the Earth, Light for the World

* 1st reading: Isaiah 58.6-10
* Psalm: 112
* 2nd reading: 1 Corinthians 2.1-5
* Gospel: Matthew 5.13-16

Jesus continues his teaching from the Sermon on the Mount. The good news that God has blessed Jesus' disciples with the kingdom of heaven is complemented with Jesus' declaration today that they are "the salt of the earth ... the light of the world".

Salt. We use it to melt ice in winter. Paired with pepper, salt is a basic seasoning. Still, many shun salt for fear of high blood pressure. In our world, salt is certainly not glamorous. Yet in the ancient world it was highly valued.

Job described the seasoning function of salt: "Can that which is tasteless be eaten without salt?" (Job 6.6). Other texts prescribed that salt be added to sacrifices (Leviticus 2.13) and declared salt mixed with incense "pure and holy" (Exodus 30.35).

Salt also symbolized the making of a friendship covenant (Numbers 18.19), and "eating salt" with someone became a pledge of loyalty (Ezra 4.14). Jesus associated salt with peace: "Have salt in yourselves, and be at peace" (Mark 9.50). Salt also represented wisdom; seasoning one's speech with salt (Colossians 4.6) meant to speak wisely.

Outside the Bible, writers told of salt's properties and benefits. The Roman writer Pliny observed, "There is nothing more useful than sunshine and salt". Diogenes Laertius said salt "should be brought to the table to remind us of what is right; for salt preserves whatever it finds and it arises from the purest sources, sun and sea".

Salt's preservative powers, then, made it one of the essentials of life. Salt purified, flavoured and enhanced that with which it made contact. Salt had a range of qualities and meanings, and we need not strain to define precisely which one the teaching of Jesus embraced. It is clear, however, that Jesus would have surprised his listeners by asserting that they, rather than the Torah, were "the salt of the earth".

In telling the disciples, "You are the salt of the earth," Jesus was not suggesting they put salt on soil. Rather, in the saying, salt serves as a metaphor and "the earth" refers to people. And just as salt functions as a preservative, preventing decay and making food tasty, so Jesus' followers are to keep society wholesome, oppose corruption and penetrate society for good. They are to ensure that life possesses zest and flavour.

Because Jesus warned his disciples about losing their savour, we need to note that salt harboured negative tones. Salt could be associated with a land gone to waste (Deuteronomy 29.23). Victors commonly sowed the land of those conquered with salt to make it uninhabitable (Judges 9.45). Because the salt of Palestine was impure, it was possible for the sodium chloride to leach out. Then salt's only fate was to be thrown out and trampled on as useless.

Light, too, is a common cultural and religious symbol. Associated with the divine, light refers to godliness or supernatural illumination. In Genesis, the Bible's first book, creation begins with God bringing light out of darkness. In the Bible's last book, when all else is past, God remains as light for the faithful (Revelation 22.5). God indeed is said to be clothed with light (Psalm 104.2) and God's face is light (Psalm 4.6).

God's communication of light to Jesus' disciples is as factual as the impossibility of hiding a city built on a hill. Yet, paradoxically, humans can hide their light under a bushel basket, though they should not. The Christian vocation is to let one's light "shine before human beings, so that they may see your good works and give glory to your Father in heaven".

Jesus' disciples are not challenged to try harder to be salt and light. Rather, as in the case of the Beatitudes, Jesus declares that his disciples are salt and light. Disciples are asked to believe Jesus' word and live out the new status he has conferred on them.

Living in this way reveals the truth Paul shares with the Corinthians: that Christian faith rests "not on human wisdom, but on the power of God" at work in them. This divine wisdom enables Christians to take up the real engagement symbolized by the religious practice of fasting – commitment to the cause of justice: "to undo the thongs of the yoke, to let the oppressed go free, and to break every yoke" (Isaiah).

Sixth Sunday in Ordinary Time

Love Fulfills and Deepens God's Commands

* 1st reading: Sirach 15.15-20
* Psalm: 119
* 2nd reading: 1 Corinthians 2.6-10
* Gospel: Matthew 5.17-37

How to reconcile human freedom and personal responsibility with God's sovereign will has long troubled religious people. The sage Ben Sira tackled this and other issues in his academy. His thoughts, recorded in the Book of Sirach, stress that men and women bear responsibility for the morality of their actions ("If you choose, you can keep the commandments, and to act faithfully is a matter of your own choice"). Each person can choose life or death ("whichever one chooses, that shall be given").

In the Sermon on the Mount, Jesus shows the way to life. This instruction is expressed by means of six antithetical statements that begin with some variation of the formula "You have heard that it was said" and conclude with Jesus' new teaching, "But I say to you".

Several of these sayings deepen the aim of a number of the Ten Commandments. Jesus forbids not only killing and adultery, but that seething anger that can lead to murder, and lustful looks, which amount to adultery in the heart.

Other sayings of Jesus radically do away with divinely permitted practices of the Old Testament world: divorce and the swearing of oaths. In effect, Jesus claims the prerogative as Son of God to re-interpret the divine commandments in the new era of the kingdom that his ministry has inaugurated.

The final two of the six "antitheses" – as they have been called – summon Jesus' followers to a non-retaliatory way of life, loving even one's enemies. We will explore the significance of this central aspect of Jesus' message (turning the other cheek; … being perfect like the heavenly Father) next week when the gospel features these sayings.

The place of Torah or law in Jewish and Christian life has been much debated through the centuries. Accordingly, Jesus has been championed as both the one who observed the Law's intent perfectly and the proponent of utter freedom towards the Law. It would seem that – paradoxically – the truth about Jesus encompasses both these views.

In principle, Jesus adhered to the Torah and was zealous about God's commands ("Do not think that I have come to abolish the Law or the Prophets; I have come not to abolish but to fulfill"). Yet, in his ministry, Jesus stressed what he called "the weightier matters of the law: justice and mercy and faith" (cf. Matthew 23.23).

ARCHBISHOP TERRENCE PRENDERGAST

Jesus cited the prophet Hosea's saying that God desired "mercy, not sacrifice" (Hosea 6.6; cf. Matthew 9.13; 12.7). Also, Jesus underlined that love of God and love of neighbour go hand in hand as features of the same Great Commandment.

"Love of one's enemies" comes as the climax of a set of instructions that plays on the motif of love of others. The first way in which love can be deepened is by not being hostile towards another (for example, not insulting a brother or sister or calling them "You fool"). Anger, Jesus says, enters into the issue of how one worships.

Curiously, however, Jesus does not address the person who is angry but the one who may have aroused anger in another. This worshipper must get his or her priorities straight: reconciliation comes before all else ("leave your gift there before the altar and go; first be reconciled to your brother or sister, and then come and offer your gift").

"Tearing out one's eye" or "cutting off one's hand or foot" are examples of hyperbolic or exaggerated speech, a typical feature of Jesus' method of teaching. One must use one's sight and limbs for God's glory, not to abuse persons made in the image and likeness of God by treating them as objects of lustful desire.

Jesus stresses the dignity of the human person. Proclaiming God's design for the marriage of men and women and radically prohibiting divorce are characteristics of Jesus' teaching that recur later in the year (Matthew 19.1-12; 25th Sunday of Ordinary Time). Finally, Jesus tells us that love demands that one's speech be utterly truthful ("Let your word be 'Yes' if 'Yes', or 'No,' if 'No'").

Paul describes the instruction Christians have received as "God's wisdom, secret and hidden". The full import of what disciples begin to learn on earth will come to completion only in heaven, for the human heart cannot now conceive "what God has prepared for those who love him".

Called to Be "Perfect" Like God

* 1st reading: Leviticus 19.1-2, 27-28
* Psalm: 103
* 2nd reading: 1 Corinthians 3.16-23
* Gospel: Matthew 5.38-48

At the Louvre Museum in Paris stands a six-foot stele on which is inscribed the Code of Hammurabi, ruler of ancient Babylon (1728–1686 BC). Besides giving us information on jurisprudence in antiquity, the Code contains the law of talion (*lex talionis*), which stipulates a strict proportion between crimes committed and punishments meted out ("an eye for an eye and a tooth for a tooth"). This law was a great advance for its time, for it proposed even-handed justice without respect to the persons implicated.

The law of talion limited retribution, ruling out any kind of vendetta so common to the ancient world and present even in our time. The Torah of Moses embraced the law of talion (cf. Exodus 21.14; Leviticus 24.20; Deuteronomy 19.21). The Holiness Code even provided the basis for doing away with vengeance ("You shall not take vengeance or bear a grudge against any of your people, but you shall love your neighbour as yourself" [Leviticus 19.18]).

When teaching about non-retaliation, Jesus told his followers not to assert their rights in personal relationships, but to put others' needs first. Jesus used exaggerated language to communicate this message. "If anyone strikes you on the right cheek, turn the other also" suggests a slap received with the back of someone's hand – not only a painful blow, but a gross insult as well.

"If anyone forces you to go one mile, go with them also the second mile" reflects the Roman habit of commandeering civilians to carry the luggage of soldiers – one of the outrages perpetrated by the occupying power. In this way, Simon of Cyrene was pressed into service, helping Jesus carry his cross (Matthew 27.32).

ARCHBISHOP TERRENCE PRENDERGAST

Enacting laws can create difficulties. The problem with the law of talion, a principle meant to limit retaliation, is that it could be invoked to justify a vindictive spirit. In the same way, an exaggeratedly literal reading of Jesus' instructions to "give to everyone who begs from you, and do not refuse anyone who wants to borrow from you" could impoverish disciples in no time.

Likewise, evil would triumph in communities where the injunction "do not resist an evildoer" – intended for personal relations – was observed slavishly.

The shocking images that Jesus proposed apply to the lives of individual disciples whose non-retaliatory behaviour invites the evildoer to be startled by the presence of the kingdom in a person's life. The enemy may then be converted to that new way of relating proposed by Jesus.

The images are not as graphic, but Jesus' commands to love one's enemies and to pray for one's persecutors constitute the most demanding aspect of his teaching. The one and only motive given is that by so doing, the disciple shares in the heavenly Father's manner of relating to the world.

For tax collectors love those who love them. And Gentiles greet their brothers and sisters. There's nothing extraordinary about that. But God "makes his sun rise on the evil and on the good, and sends rain on the righteous and on the unrighteous". God simply gives. To be like God, one must be a giver. There are limits, of course. Otherwise, Christians would suffer burnout or be deprived of the resources they need to live, work and contribute to the kingdom.

Wise Christians know that the two-fold Great Commandment involves loving God with all one's being and loving one's neighbour *as one loves oneself*. In truth, one loves one's neighbour only when one loves oneself.

When used to describe God, the word "perfect" can mean "mature", "fully grown" or "blameless". It seems to mean the same as "holy" in the Book of Leviticus ("You shall be holy, for I the Lord your God am holy").

Jesus' teaching points to the full implications of loving: namely, coming thereby to share in the perfection of God's life, which consists in constant self-donation, selfless giving.

Paul tells the Corinthians, indwelt by God's Spirit, that they have become – each and every one – God's temple ("God's temple is holy, and you are that temple").

Though poor or thought to be fools, Christ's followers paradoxically possess all things present and to come ("all [things] belong to you"). For the Christian knows that he or she belongs to Christ, "and Christ belongs to God".

Eighth Sunday in Ordinary Time

Living Without Anxiety as a Steward

* 1st reading: Isaiah 49.14-15
* Psalm: 62
* 2nd reading: 1 Corinthians 4.1-5
* Gospel: Matthew 6.24-34

The notion of providence – literally, God's "foreseeing" of one's needs – receives too little consideration today. Weather maps, economic forecasting and technological control are so commonplace in our lives that we do not move past secondary causes to find God in our world.

So the injunctions of Jesus in the gospel – to put aside anxiety and trust the Heavenly Father – can be a challenge for modern disciples. This invitation, "do not worry", is a leitmotif of Jesus' message, appearing six times in the passage (6.25, 27, 28, 31 and 34 [twice]).

The invitation to trust in God's providence does not eliminate one's need to work or own property. After all, Jesus directed his

ARCHBISHOP TERRENCE PRENDERGAST

message to people involved in the agricultural tasks he mentioned: sowing, reaping, storing in barns, toiling and spinning.

Still, all are challenged to understand that their lives cannot be based on such things. Individuals are not to live as birds or lilies, but rather to note that God's care touches every aspect of creation, including birds, lilies and human beings.

Jesus suggests that the way to live without anxiety or worry is to put things in their proper order, by first of all seeking God's kingdom and its righteousness. Then, Jesus pledges, "all these things [food and drink and clothing] will be given to you as well" [by the Heavenly Father].

The first reading, from Isaiah, notes how unlikely it would be for a mother to forget the child she carried in her womb. The prophet argues how much more unlikely it is, then, that God would forget his children.

God wants his children to know that life is "more than food" and "the body more than clothing". Indeed, God cares for human beings made in his image and likeness more than for the birds of the air and the lilies of the field, upon which God lavishes nurture and vesture.

Worry or anxiety, Jesus pleads, cannot add an hour to one's span of life, and tomorrow will bring its own worries. So one should not worry about tomorrow, only about today!

This does not mean one ought not to plan for the future. Jesus' message is meant to be reassuring: let each follower of the Lord address each day's problems as they come, confident that one's life is in the hands of a loving Father.

What works against this spiritual disposition, Jesus suggests at the outset, is a divided heart, trying to serve two masters: God and something else.

Now the symbol for what is other than God is here said to be "wealth" or, perhaps better, "wealth's sway". The Aramaic word underlying this other possible "lord" is "Mammon", which is simply another word for "property", including, but not limited to, money. In itself, Mammon has no sinister connotations, but it can stand for anything human that one serves as something that gives meaning to one's life. The choice is not whether one will serve, but what or whom one will serve – God or another person, thing or cause.

When Paul speaks of his ministry, he introduces a term that is helpful in viewing one's life as a disciple: the notion of being a steward. Paul speaks of Christians having become "servants of Christ" and "stewards" to whom God's mysteries have been entrusted.

In 1990, the bishops of the United States wrote a pastoral letter entitled "Stewardship: A Disciple's Response". The letter suggested that the biblical ideal of a "steward" was a good way to envision what it means to be a disciple in our time.

Stewards are people amazed by, and grateful for, what they have been given by God. They find it awesome that a measure of years has been allotted to an individual, along with a unique combination of skills and abilities, and that through the coming together of abilities, good fortune and time they have been able to earn material wealth or possessions far beyond anything that they might have imagined!

Stewards know that they did not earn their time, talents or treasure. Rather, these are gifts of a generous God who asks only that his children be grateful and, in their turn, generous, too.

Paul says that a steward needs to be trustworthy. Paul thinks that faithfulness and trustworthiness can be demonstrated by consistent performance over time. This is a record that, by God's grace and his response, Paul was able to establish with the Corinthians to God's praise and glory.

Ninth Sunday in Ordinary Time

The Righteousness of God

* 1st reading: Deuteronomy 11.18, 26-28, 32
* Psalm: 31
* 2nd reading: Romans 3.21-25, 28
* Gospel: Matthew 7.21-27

A recurring theme and debate among believers concerns the nature of salvation. How is one saved? What role does God play? What is the human person's contribution? These issues come to the fore as disciples of Christ ponder the Scriptures proposed in this Sunday's liturgy.

In the closing verses of Deuteronomy 11 – the completion of the hortatory introduction (4.1–11.32) – Moses invites Israelites on the cusp of entering the Promised Land to possess it, dwell in it and live there in accord with God's covenant love, obeying the statutes and ordinances he proclaims in their hearing (chapters 12–26). To do this would mean inheriting a blessing; to fail to do so would be to live under a curse coming on all who do not obey God's commandments.

Something similar seems to be at work in the closing words of Jesus' Sermon on the Mount (Matthew 5.1–7.27). Jesus warns those who call on him as Lord and do mighty works (prophesying in his name, casting out demons and doing deeds of power [miracles] in his name), but fail to do the will of the Heavenly Father, that he will disown them on the Day of Judgment ("on that day"). He will say, "I never knew you; get away from me, you evildoers".

There follows a parable about two kinds of house-builders to illustrate the difference between those who hear Jesus' words and put them into practice and those who hear his words but do not act upon them.

The first kind of people resemble a wise man who built his house on rock. The house was able to withstand rain, floods and fierce winds. The latter folk are like a foolish man whose house collapsed at the onslaught of falling rain, floods and wind because it was built on sand.

The conclusion to the Sermon is like Moses' setting before the Israelites the choice of a blessing or a curse.

Indeed, both passages seem to suggest that if people just set their minds and hearts to it, they can keep God's commandments or observe Jesus' teaching and so be saved. They can live with a divine blessing rather than a curse, or, in the words of the gospel, "enter the kingdom of heaven".

By contrast with this seeming emphasis on the capacity of human beings to achieve the blessing or to enter the divine realm, Paul carries on a polemic against such a concept by boldly proclaiming in a key paragraph of the Letter to the Romans, "We hold that a person is justified by faith apart from [the doing of] works prescribed by the Law" (Romans 3.28).

This principle parallels the equally strong emphasis in the opening of today's second reading: "now, apart from [a person's keeping of the] Law, the righteousness of God has been disclosed".

Finally, a key phrase stresses the utter gratuity of God's bestowal of righteousness on sinners who are unable to save themselves. Paul asserts that all who have fallen short of the glory of God "are now justified by his grace as a gift".

Paul speaks about how God effected this redemption for humankind, which is unable to achieve it on its own. He says, "God put forward [Jesus Christ] as a sacrifice of atonement by his blood".

This very complex thought structure claims that all the sacrifices of the past were ineffective: that is, they could not make sinners right with God. So the Lord took matters into his own hands once the Israelites, along with the Gentiles, had fallen into estrangement with God by sinful disobedience.

Indeed, God made Jesus into the new "mercy seat" (the place on the ark of the covenant in the Jerusalem Temple where the high priest sprinkled the blood of sacrifice) so as to make believers righteous. In another passage, Paul says that "For our sake, [God] made [Jesus] to be [an offering for] sin who knew no sin, so that in him we might become the righteousness of God" (2 Corinthians 5.21).

What Christians can now do is to respond in gratitude for the gift of salvation by letting the Holy Spirit guide them as righteous believers into keeping God's commandments, to heeding and following Jesus' teaching.

So then, God's initiative in freely giving salvation to sinners needs to be seen as the starting-point. Afterwards comes the forgiven disciple's cooperation with God's grace, that is, living in accordance to the divine commandments (love of God and love of neighbour).

Entering into Lent with Jesus

* 1st reading: Genesis 2.7-9, 16-18, 25; 3.1-7
* Psalm: 51
* 2nd reading: Romans 5.12-19
* Gospel: Matthew 4.1-11

The Sundays of Lent this year feature the archetypal images of each Christian's relationship with Jesus. On the first two Sundays, disciples re-experience their Lord's conquest of the temptations in the desert and his mystical conversation with Moses and Elijah on the Mount of Transfiguration.

The next three Sundays invite believers to share Jesus' encounters with people like themselves: the Samaritan woman at the well, the man born blind, and Jesus' friend Lazarus, who was raised from the tomb. Then comes the climax of Holy Week and the central events of Christian faith – the paschal mystery – Jesus' passion, death and resurrection.

Lent is about each Christian's rediscovery and reappropriation of the death to sin and rising to new life that took place when he or she was baptized into Christ Jesus.

The first Lenten preface puts this well, praising God for personal transformation: "As we recall the great events that gave us new life in Christ, You bring the image of Your Son to perfection within us".

How can one best enter into Lent with Jesus? Primarily, by sharing in the daily Eucharist, which has long been a favoured Catholic way of observing Lent.

Those for whom daily Mass is not possible may wish to substitute a daily reading from the word of God. Jesus says in today's gospel, "[One] does not live by bread alone, but by every word that comes from the mouth of God".

One could reflect on the Sunday readings throughout the week or else meditate for a few minutes each day on the Scripture readings for the Lenten weekdays. Some might prefer to read continuously through a gospel or other biblical book (the Gospels of Matthew and John are apt this year). Especially in the latter part of Lent, the Sorrowful Mysteries of the Rosary and the Way of the Cross help us keep the passion of Jesus in mind.

Besides prayer, Lenten practices have always included fasting and almsgiving. The Church prescribes fasting and abstinence from meat on Ash Wednesday and Good Friday; abstinence is recommended on the other Fridays of Lent.

Money saved by these and other acts of self-denial are given to the poor in a gesture of solidarity with "the least of Jesus' brothers and sisters" (the Church's Lenten charitable appeal being privileged recipients): "You ask us to express our thanks by self-denial ...; we are to show to those in need your goodness to ourselves" (Lenten preface III).

Genesis depicts man and woman in a garden in Eden, surrounded with abundance. In primal innocence they are unashamed of their nakedness. God, who had breathed the breath of life into their nostrils, gave them access to all the fruits of the earth with one restriction – that they not eat "of the tree of the knowledge of good and evil".

The Bible says God does not "tempt" humans but "tests" them to see what is in their hearts. Temptation can come at the hands of several figures: "Satan", "the Devil", the "Prince of This World" are some of the personal titles given to God's enemy.

Forces opposed to God are sometimes put in impersonal terms: "the lust of the flesh and the lust of the eyes and the pride of life" (1 John 1.16). In effect, all of these forces try to drive a wedge between people and God so that they are tempted not to trust God.

The man and the woman did not resist the Tempter's blandishments. They yielded to the desire to "be like God" and disobeyed God's commandment. By contrast, Jesus resisted three unworthy ways of being the "Son of God" proposed by the devil: using his power to satisfy hunger rather than for the good of others; "tempting" God to care for him by casting himself down from the pinnacle of the Temple; worshipping Satan to gain worldly power and prestige.

Jesus' vocation was to fulfill his divine Sonship by dying on the cross in obedience to the Father. No other way was worthy of him. Scripture armed Jesus with the resources to thwart the devil ("Away with you, Satan!"). Scripture provides the disciple with the means to trust God more profoundly and to overcome temptation in Christ's manner and with his help.

Second Sunday of Lent

On the Mount of Transfiguration with Jesus

* 1st reading: Genesis 12.1-4
* Psalm: 33
* 2nd reading: 2 Timothy 1.8b-10
* Gospel: Matthew 17.1-9

Today's Genesis reading tells of the beginning of God's involve-ment with humanity in what has become known as "salva-tion history". Here we read the story of a divine summons issued to Abram and of the exciting divine-human encounters that followed.

God's call was met with faith when this man and his family left homeland, relatives and possessions ("Go from your country and your kindred and your father's house to the land that I will show you"). They journeyed into the unknown and the unfamiliar, trust-ing in a promise God had made ("I will make of you a great nation, and I will bless you, and make your name great, so that you will be a blessing"). On the journey God changed Abram's name to Abraham, "the father of a multitude" (Genesis 17.5).

Abraham's posterity – through Isaac and Jacob-Israel – grew and prospered until famine forced them to go to Egypt, where they fell into servitude. Afflicted with much suffering at the hand of Pharaoh, they cried out to the Lord for relief. God then raised up Moses to rescue them from the yoke of the Egyptians in the Exodus.

After God led Israel out of bondage in Egypt, they wandered in the wilderness and came to the mountain of God, which is called Sinai in some traditions, Horeb in others. There God fashioned a covenant with the people, who committed themselves to observe God's commandments. Newly bonded, Israel became known as God's children.

Last week's gospel recalled Jesus' temptations in the wilderness. In the desert, Israel had proved disobedient, lacking trust in God. By contrast, Jesus was totally obedient, entrusting himself to God's will manifest in the Scriptures. The Transfiguration story situates Jesus on a mountaintop; in it we find echoes of the Sinai revelation as well as striking differences.

Matthew's account of the Transfiguration (in comparison with Mark's version) mentions Moses before Elijah. Perhaps this word order emphasizes Jesus' status as a new Moses. To the detail that the garments of Jesus became "dazzling white", Matthew adds "and his face shone like the sun". This phrase may be meant to recall a detail mentioned in Exodus 34.29-35, which says that Moses' face "shone" because he had been talking with God. Incidentally, like Moses, Elijah conversed with God on the holy mountain.

Matthew contains a minor narrative detail, describing the cloud that covered Jesus and his heavenly companions as "bright". This detail produces the paradox that a bright cloud overshadows. Matthew may be alluding to the *Shekinah*, the cloud of God's glory that used to fill the tabernacle of God's presence in the wilderness.

The radiance of Jesus' face suggests that the Transfiguration represents the breaking through into history of Jesus' glory as God's Son. Or else it affords a glimpse of the glory that will belong to Jesus when he brings salvation to completion at the Parousia (second coming).

In Matthew's account, God's message in the voice from the cloud is more extensive. In addition to "This is my beloved Son" (found in Mark's account), we find the words "with him I am well pleased". This is an echo of Isaiah 42.1, present also in the synoptic accounts of Jesus' baptism. Not only is Jesus like Moses, Jesus is greater than Moses; and Jesus surpasses Elijah, the biblical representative of prophecy.

Another touch found only in Matthew's narrative concerns the way Jesus deals with his frightened disciples. "Jesus came and touched them, saying, 'Get up and do not be afraid'". Jesus pointed out to them that they would not grasp and should not speak about the vision they have seen "until after the Son of Man has been raised from the dead".

The Preface for the Second Sunday of Lent uses other words to explain the purpose of the Transfiguration. Though Jesus had already prepared the disciples for his approaching death, "he wanted to teach them that the promised Christ had first to suffer and so come to the glory of his resurrection".

Christians need encouragement and support so that, as Paul puts it, they can join "in suffering for the Gospel, relying on the power of God, who saved us ... according to his own purpose and grace". This may be why every Lenten journey with Jesus includes a stop at the Mount of Transfiguration.

Third Sunday of Lent

Joining Jesus' Conversation with the Samaritan Woman

* 1st reading: Exodus 17.3-7
* Psalm: 95
* 2nd reading: Romans 5.1-2, 5-8
* Gospel: John 4.5-42

Jesus' encounter with the woman of Samaria is a drama in several acts that has fascinated Christians through the ages. Interpreters in different eras have differed over whom she stands for and what we are to make of several features in the story. It is impossible to mention all the details, so we will consider only a few in the hope that these may lead the Christian reader into the depths of this profound text.

Some have seen this feisty woman as a heretic (all Samaritans were so viewed by Jews); others considered her the model of the truly spiritual person (Jesus reveals to her that one day people will not worship on Mount Gerizim, the Samaritan holy place, or in Jerusalem, the Jewish holy place).

Indeed, in the next breath Jesus told her that that day had arrived even as they were speaking ("the hour is coming, and is now here, when the true worshippers will worship the Father in spirit and truth").

In dialogue, Jesus described the woman's marital status, revealing that he knew she had had five husbands and that the man she currently was living with was not her husband. Later on, she interpreted this to her townsfolk in this way: "Come and see a man who told me everything I have ever done. He cannot be the Messiah, can he?"

Jesus' revelation of her life to the woman and his acceptance of her led her to ask about spiritual matters and then to make a leading assertion that probed into his identity ("When [the Messiah] comes, he will proclaim all things to us"). Jesus' answer was straightforward: "I am he", a phrase that echoes throughout the Fourth Gospel.

When Jesus' disciples returned, they were astonished that he had violated societal conventions of the day. A Jewish man did not initiate a conversation with an unknown woman, nor did a Jewish teacher engage in public conversation with a woman. Moreover, Jews did not invite contact with Samaritans for fear of ritual contamination.

But the disciples kept quiet about their puzzlement, and the reader learns that "the woman left her water jar and went back to the city". As Jesus and the disciples discussed the food he had that they knew nothing about ("My food is to do the will of him who sent

ARCHBISHOP TERRENCE PRENDERGAST

me"), the abandoned water jar suggests that the woman's desire for "living water" was surpassed by her recognition of Jesus' identity.

Food and drink on the human level become symbols of human longing and search for eternal life. Jesus gives this to people through the life-giving Spirit ("the water that I will give ... will become [in them] a spring of water gushing up to eternal life"). This symbolism may also touch on the woman's search for meaning and significant relationships in life.

At the end of the drama, the woman of Samaria has become an evangelist, bringing her neighbours, by means of her testimony, to meet Jesus and beg him to "stay with them". After two days they come to faith "because of his word", confessing him to be "truly the Saviour of the world".

In commenting on the Gospel of John, St. Augustine said of the Samaritan woman, "Let us hear ourselves in her, let us recognize ourselves in her, and, in her, let us give thanks to God for ourselves". Each Christian will identify with different features of the narrative, but all are invited to the same openness she displayed to being questioned and challenged by Jesus as she was.

The reading from Exodus touches on the thirst of the People of God for water. There, however, thirst led not to faith but to doubt and rebellion. Despite their rebellion, God was gracious, giving the Israelites water from the rock through Moses' intervention.

In the letter to the Romans, Paul argues that human yearning for reconciliation has been met through God's love for sinful humanity, manifest in the fact that "while we were still sinners Christ died for us". It is through the saving mystery of the cross that God has slaked all human thirst by pouring divine love "into our hearts through the Holy Spirit that has been given to us".

Fourth Sunday of Lent

Facing up to One's Blindness

* 1st reading: 1 Samuel 16.1b, 6-7, 10-13
* Psalm: 23
* 2nd reading: Ephesians 5.8-14
* Gospel: John 9.1-41

In the Gnostic heresy at Ephesus, Paul faced "enlightened" people who felt they were "above" a distinction such as the one between good and evil deeds. Quoting what is possibly part of an ancient baptismal hymn, the apostle reminds Christian disciples that falling into the clutches of sin means being given over to the sleep of death, out of which Christ awakens them by the light of his glorious resurrection ("Sleeper, awake! Rise from the dead, and Christ will shine on you").

In their sinful past, Christians belonged to darkness, but now "in the Lord [they] are light". And they are called to live as children of light ("the fruit of the light is found in all that is good and right and true"). The gospel story of the man blind from birth explores the themes of light and darkness under the images of blindness and recovery of sight; unbelief and coming to faith; sin and truly living righteously.

The introduction to the story of the healing of the man blind from birth shows that Jesus' disciples make the error – common even among long-time Christians – of associating a misfortune suffered with some supposed sin. "What did I do that God should be punishing me like this?" they ask.

Imagining that the blind man could have sinned even in the womb, his disciples asked Jesus, "Rabbi, who sinned, this man or his parents, that he was born blind?" Rejecting any connection between sin and the man's blindness, Jesus said, "He was born blind so that God's works might be revealed in him". This prepares the reader for

ARCHBISHOP TERRENCE PRENDERGAST

the man's healing but also suggests that God can draw good from an illness or from human suffering.

Jesus performed an external ritual, making a paste out of his saliva and some earth. Then he sent the man to the Pool of Siloam, a name that the Evangelist interprets to mean "Sent". Sent, the man was engaged and challenged by the command of Jesus. We can scarcely imagine what he was thinking about as he stumbled to Siloam en route to his healing.

The narrative following the healing introduces the reader to the religious authorities of that day, who were sceptical about Jesus because he made the paste for the man's eyes on a Sabbath, and to the man's parents, who were non-committal when pressed about how he came to see ("Ask him; he is of age").

However, the story's focus falls on the man blind from birth. Emboldened by his healing, he began to draw conclusions about Jesus:

"How can a man who is a sinner perform such signs?"

"He is a Prophet."

"Here is an astonishing thing! ... Never since the world began has it been heard that anyone opened the eyes of a person born blind. If this man were not from God, he could do nothing".

There remained, of course, one more step to be taken. Jesus initiated it by asking him whether he believed in the Son of Man, then identifying himself as this mysterious figure from God. The man confessed, "'Lord, I believe'. And he worshipped him".

We learn that Jesus wants to lead people to see not only physically but with the eyes of faith. This the newly sighted man does, while others prefer to persevere in their spiritual blindness. The challenge Jesus poses to each Christian is to face his or her own interior blindness (whatever form it might take) and to grow in faith. This is the challenge that the story of the man blind from birth poses for Christians along their Lenten journey.

David's anointing by Saul illustrates the principle that "the Lord does not see as the humans see". While human beings have the tendency to judge on externals, "the Lord looks on the heart". God chose David and his heirs – including Christ – to rule over his people.

God's designs are sovereign. And the mystery of divine election – why God chose David or why Jesus healed the man blind from birth but not others – remains just that, a mystery.

The liturgy summarizes this mystery of God's ongoing choice of new members for his holy people: Jesus came "to lead us from darkness into the light of faith" (Preface for the Fourth Sunday of Lent).

Fifth Sunday of Lent

Jesus Weeps at the Death of His Friend Lazarus

* 1st reading: Ezekiel 37.12-14
* Psalm: 130
* 2nd reading: Romans 8.8-11
* Gospel: John 11.1-45

Death is perhaps the most painful of human experiences. Not only facing one's own death, but also the death of a loved one: a spouse, a child, a friend. When death intrudes into human life, it evokes powerful emotions (anger, astonishment, fear, recrimination). All of these – and issues of faith – underlie the narrative of Jesus' raising of Lazarus.

Only a fraction of the story actually deals with Lazarus' illness and death (John 11.1-5, 38-44). The major part of this long narrative consists of Jesus' conversations with his disciples (verses 7-16) and with Martha and Mary, the sisters of Lazarus (verses 20-37).

At the centre of the episode lies Jesus' declaration to Mary that "I am the resurrection and the life. Those who believe in me, even though they die, will live, and everyone who lives and believes in me will never die".

ARCHBISHOP TERRENCE PRENDERGAST

The Fourth Evangelist's storytelling method aims at making an emotional impact on the reader. John keeps the reader in suspense with one delaying tactic after another: having Jesus wait after news of Lazarus' illness until he can declare "Lazarus is dead"; separate meetings with each of the sisters; dwelling on the emotions of Jesus; Jesus' prayer to his Father at the tomb. Lazarus' emergence from the tomb startles the reader or hearer and provokes reflection on Jesus' identity.

Jesus' strong emotions have caused interpreters a great deal of difficulty, to the point that they generally soften these emotions in translation. The Greek verb that John used to describe Jesus' anger can refer to the snorting of horses. When applied to human beings, it hints at outrage, anger, a troubled spirit or emotional indignation. John suggests that Jesus was outraged and agitated; the liturgical translation attenuates this somewhat ("he was greatly disturbed in spirit and deeply moved").

But why did Jesus react so strongly? Not only was he powerfully moved interiorly, "Jesus began to weep". Some feel Jesus' tears cannot be for Lazarus' fate or only because of his friendship with Lazarus, for Jesus was about to raise Lazarus from the tomb. Jesus' strong feelings and tears may be his reaction to the unbelief of those who surrounded him. They may equally constitute Jesus' acknowledgement of the burden of pain that death inflicts on human life.

Jesus' final act before raising Lazarus was a prayer to his Father, expressing gratitude that God hears his prayer ("Father, I thank you for having heard me. I knew that you always hear me"). The Father has entrusted to Jesus power over life and death. This is the last great revelation of the gospel. It serves as a corollary to the Father's command that Jesus lay down his life and take it up again (John 10.18).

Coming after the restoration of the blind man's sight, with which it is closely associated ("Could not he who opened the eyes of the blind man have kept this man from dying?"), Jesus' raising of Lazarus shows that Jesus offers light and life to all.

The prophet Ezekiel's vision of the Valley of Dry Bones is one of the most famous passages from this book (37.1-14). God pledges to cover these bones with sinews, flesh and skin and to give each of them individually the breath of new life.

The interpretation of the vision (37.12-14) applies it to the House of Israel, which was despairing, broken in spirit and bereft of hope. The Church has applied the vision to Jesus' resurrection or to the general resurrection at the end of time. It comments appropriately on the raising of Lazarus because his restoration to life – a resuscitation rather than a resurrection – anticipates, though in limited fashion, Jesus' own resurrection.

Paul speaks of the way death and life are intermingled in Christian life: "If Christ is in you, though the body is dead because of sin, the Spirit is life because of righteousness". Yes, Christians will die as a result of the consequences which sin works in their lives.

This is not God's last word, however. Rather, in the end God will share Christ's triumph with his disciples ("[God] who raised Christ from the dead will give life to your mortal bodies also through his Spirit that dwells in you").

Palm Sunday of the Lord's Passion

The Glory and Agony of Holy Week

* Gospel: Matthew 21.1-11
* 1st reading: Isaiah 50.4-7
* Psalm: 22
* 2nd reading: Philippians 2.6-11
* Gospel: Matthew 26.14–27.66

The liturgical texts of Passion Sunday are incomparably rich; it is scarcely possible to do them justice in so brief a treatment. The Isaiah passage is the third of four poems known as "Songs of the (Suffering) Servant"; it tells of the humility of God's end-time servant, whom Christians have identified with Jesus.

Qualifying Jesus' humility with selflessness, in Philippians Paul quoted an early Christian hymn extolling Jesus' obedience "to the point of death", possibly adding the words "even death on a cross".

ARCHBISHOP TERRENCE PRENDERGAST

Two gospel passages are read today: the Matthean Passion narrative and the account of Jesus' dramatic entry into Jerusalem. Jesus entered Jerusalem humbly, seated on a lowly beast of burden and accepting the crowd's acclaim of him as messianic king. God oversaw this entry (as God guided the entire passion), which was in fulfillment of prophecy.

As he often does, Matthew shows how two scriptural texts read together (Isaiah 62.11 and Zechariah 9.9) presaged Jesus' activity of riding into the Holy City humbly as a servant and not, as some anticipated, as a warrior on a stallion.

Jesus came to die and to inaugurate salvation within a kingdom that is universal in scope, one transcending any limited visions the religious leaders, the crowds or Jesus' disciples might have had.

Matthew's sequence of Jesus' last days and hours is much like Mark's. But there are striking nuances in Matthew that differ from those found in Mark's treatment. For instance, only Matthew tells of Judas Iscariot's remorse over his role in handing Jesus over to the religious leaders and of an intervention made by Pilate's wife declaring Jesus' innocence ("Have nothing to do with that innocent man, for today I have suffered a great deal because of a dream about him").

In the "words of institution" at the Last Supper, Matthew and Mark reflect a Palestinian Jewish tradition concerning Jesus' self-offering in the Eucharist. They see the Eucharist as the renewed expression of the covenant God made with Israel in Exodus 24.6-8 ("the Blood of the covenant, which is poured out for many").

Still, only Matthew recounts Jesus' interpretive words that his death was "for the forgiveness of sins" (Matthew 26.28). Foreshadowed in the breaking of bread and the sharing of the cup of wine that he declared to be his Body and Blood, Jesus' death effects the forgiveness of the world's sins, thereby creating a new order of relationships with God. The Eucharist is linked to Calvary, making the fruits of Jesus' death and resurrection available to those who believe and approach Jesus' sacramental existence with faith in his Real Presence.

Mark's version of the prayer of Jesus in the Garden of Gethsemane focused on Jesus' agony and the disciples' inability to console him.

While Matthew was aware of these features ("Are you still sleeping and taking your rest? See, the hour is at hand, and the Son of Man is betrayed into the hands of sinners"), he depicted Jesus as totally submissive to God, modelling faith-filled prayer ("My Father, if it is possible, let this cup pass from me; yet not what I want, but what you want" and "My Father, if this cannot pass unless I drink it, your will be done").

Jesus' prayer from the cross, "My God, my God, why have you forsaken me?" (the opening words of Psalm 22) has troubled some of his followers. No explanation can soften the realization that the human Jesus died with a cry of anguish and abandonment on his lips. Yet he did not despair. In his pain, Jesus uttered a lament to his Father, whom he addressed as "my God". Jesus' cry to God was one of trust.

This is also the conclusion reached by reading Psalm 22 in its entirety. For it closes with a pledge to sing God's praises in the assembly after rescue from the clutches of death ("I will tell of your name to my brothers and sisters; in the midst of the congregation, I will praise you").

Matthew's account of Jesus' death features an earthquake. Thereby he signals that the resurrection does not negate Jesus' suffering and death. The evangelist intimates that, instead, God breaks into the human world to transform it, a theme of the Easter season, which is about to begin.

Easter Sunday

The Shattering Experience of Jesus' Resurrection

* 1st reading: Acts 10.34a, 37-43
* Psalm: 118
* 2nd reading: 1 Corinthians 3.1-4 (or Colossians 5.6b-8)
* Gospel: John 20.1-18 (or 20.1-9) – to be treated in the Commentary in Year B; Matthew 28.1-10 (from the Vigil); or, in the evening, Luke 24.13-35 (see Easter Sunday 3A)

ARCHBISHOP TERRENCE PRENDERGAST

For the evangelist Matthew, the paschal mystery – the death and resurrection of Jesus viewed as a whole – was a shattering experience. At the death of Jesus, a great earthquake took place, powerfully communicating Jesus' victory over death (Matthew 27.54). Another earthquake preceded the proclamation of Jesus' resurrection to the faithful women at the tomb.

God's fulfillment of Old Testament promises in the glory of the risen Jesus serves as a key for comprehending the Scripture passages of the Easter Vigil and the early Church's proclamation of Jesus' resurrection in the Acts of the Apostles. As Peter put it, "All the Prophets testify about [Jesus] that everyone who believes in him receives forgiveness of sins through his name".

Matthew differs from Mark and Luke over the purpose of the women's visit to the tomb. For Matthew, the women went to the grave not to anoint the body of Jesus but "to see the tomb". They wanted to ascertain, according to Jewish custom, that Jesus had truly died. There may be a touch of irony, then, in the way in which Matthew opens his Easter story.

As commentators have pointed out, no one was an eyewitness to the resurrection. With the earthquake, Matthew symbolized Jesus' resurrection breaking into the static world of human beings. God's glory became visible in the angel's appearance ("like lightning, and his clothing white as snow") and powerful intervention ("an Angel of the Lord ... rolled back the stone and sat on it"), as well as in the utter fear that came over the guards ("the guards shook and became like dead men"). Clearly, God was at work in raising Jesus from death.

While the resurrection's impact was awesome, its divine purpose was to offer a blessing to people. Accordingly, the angel twice appealed to the women not to yield to fear ("Do not be afraid") and interpreted the cataclysmic events for them ("He is not here; for he has been raised, as he said"). The angel also commanded – a feature prominent in the resurrection narratives – that what God has done in raising Jesus be proclaimed to others ("go quickly and tell his disciples").

The angel's interpretive word referred to the crucifixion in the Greek perfect tense. This past tense indicates that the completed events of Jesus' cross and resurrection continue to have implications now. So, Jesus remains forever the "Crucified One"; his atoning death continues to bring salvation to all who believe. As well, Jesus remains for all time the Risen One, communicating eternal life to those who follow in his way. In his glorified state, Jesus shares the ongoing dimension of his death and risen life with others in such a way as to transform their lives ("Our paschal lamb, Christ has been sacrificed. Therefore, let us celebrate the festival ... with the unleavened bread of sincerity and truth").

While the empty tomb can be explained in various ways (the theft of Jesus' body by his disciples or others – cf. Matthew 27.64; 28.13), faith demands that the truth of Jesus' resurrection be corroborated by the empty grave ("He is not here").

The angel promised that the disciples would encounter Jesus again ("he is going ahead of you to Galilee; there you will see him"). Though the Greek word for "seeing" is different from that used in the opening verse, Matthew may have been contrasting the beginning of the story from its conclusion. On a Sabbath in Jerusalem, the women went to see a tomb and the realm of death; by God's doing, on a new day in Galilee the disciples will see Jesus in his risen glory.

Though a future meeting in Galilee was promised, the grace and peace of the resurrection could not be kept under wraps till then. Suddenly, Jesus appeared to the women, offering "greetings" of peace and reiterating the angel's Easter command "to tell my brothers to go to Galilee".

Drawing near, the women clasped Jesus' feet and worshipped him – a surrender of themselves befitting the new era inaugurated by the resurrection. In his risen life, Jesus Christ receives the obedient worship of women and men (cf. Matthew 28.17), who bow down in the name of the whole of creation, which has been made new.

Second Sunday of Easter

The Risen Jesus Shares His Spirit and Joy

* 1st reading: Acts 2.42-47
* Psalm: 118
* 2nd reading: 1 Peter 1.3-9
* Gospel: John 20.19-31

The Church invites Christians to celebrate the mystery of the resurrection for the Great Fifty Days leading to Pentecost. This chronology – which separates the early Church's experience of the Risen Lord's presence into discrete moments (Jesus' resurrection, ascension and gift of the Spirit) – owes much to the schema Luke presents in the Acts of the Apostles.

The Fourth Gospel, for its part, stresses the underlying unity of these same mysteries of the risen Lord Jesus Christ. Thus, today's gospel notes that on the evening of the day of his resurrection ("the first day of the week"), Jesus conferred the Spirit on the disciples ("Receive the Holy Spirit") and the authority to forgive sins in Jesus' name ("If you forgive the sins of any, they are forgiven them; if you retain the sins of any, they are retained").

In John the Evangelist's perspective, Jesus' new, risen life, the conferral of the Spirit and the proclamation and celebration of the forgiveness of sins are all intimately connected. Though it is not explicitly stated, John implies that Jesus' ascension to the Father took place on Easter Day soon after his encounter with Mary Magdalene in the garden.

Implied in the Church's exercising of the authority Jesus carried out in his ministry is the conviction that the Church possesses from the Holy Spirit power to discern whose sins are to be forgiven and whose retained. The Holy Spirit helps the Church recognize whose hearts have been moved by hearing the good news of the kingdom to accept God's love and forgiveness.

In *Bound to Forgive*, a book recounting his years of captivity in Beirut (Ave Maria Press, 1995), the American Servite Lawrence Jenco explores the way the activities of forgiving and forgetting are connected.

"Some people advise me to forgive and forget", the late Fr. Jenco writes. "They do not realize that this is almost impossible. Jesus, the wounded healer asks us to forgive, but he does not ask us to forget. That would be amnesia. He does demand we heal our memories .... Having forgiven, I am liberated. I need no longer be determined by the past. I move into the future free to imagine new possibilities" (p. 135).

The account of Jesus' meeting with Thomas explores this notion of the healing of memories. When the disciples told him of their meeting with Jesus ("We have seen the Lord"), Thomas could remember only Jesus' suffering and death ("Unless I see the mark of the nails in his hands, and put my finger in the mark of the nails and my hand in his side, I will not believe").

In a way, Thomas has done believers of subsequent generations – and prone to his outlook – a service. Thomas's doubt raises the issue of the link between seeing and believing. In his gentle handling of Thomas, we can see how Jesus addresses the doubts, fears and concerns of disciples ("Reach out your hand and put it in my side. Do not doubt but believe").

The challenge to believe evokes from Thomas a most profound expression of faith in Jesus' identity ("My Lord and my God!"). It is a prayer that has found a place on the lips of Christians down the ages. And Jesus' rejoinder describes the joy shared by Christians who, though they have not seen Jesus in the flesh, yet believe in him ("Blessed are those who have not seen and yet have come to believe.").

In the second reading, Peter picks up on the Christian of today's relationship with Christ. "Although you have not seen him, you love him; and even though you do not see him now, you believe in him and rejoice with an indescribable and glorious joy ...".

ARCHBISHOP TERRENCE PRENDERGAST

This joy Peter described is a fruit of the Spirit at work in Christians in every age. It prompted the early Church to have "all things in common", sharing their possessions. This simplicity and joy of the Jerusalem community has often proven a model for Church renewal. "They broke bread together at home and ate their food with glad and generous hearts, praising God and having the goodwill of all the people. And day by day the Lord added to their number those who were being saved."

Third Sunday of Easter

"Were Not Our Hearts Burning Within Us?"

* 1st reading: Acts 2.14, 22b-28
* Psalm: 16
* 2nd reading: 1 Peter 1.17-21
* Gospel: Luke 24.13-35

Visitors to the Holy Land seeking the village of Emmaus find several sites vying for the honour. This is because the manuscript tradition differs on its distance from Jerusalem. Some versions read 60 stadia (about 11 kilometres), others 160 stadia (about 30 kilometres). The fact that Emmaus cannot be located invites Christians to contemplate its spiritual meaning.

In *The Magnificent Defeat* (Seabury, 1966), Frederick Buechner described Emmaus as "the place we go in order to escape – a bar, a movie, wherever it is we throw up our hands and say, 'Let the whole damned thing go hang. It makes no difference anyway'" (p. 85). Echoes of this sentiment are found in Luke's account of the risen Jesus' meeting with two disciples bound for Emmaus, trying to forget harsh realities.

As they journeyed, Cleopas and his unnamed companion (his wife?) conversed "about all these things that had happened". Though they were joined by Jesus, "their eyes were kept from recognizing him".

Jesus initiated the conversation with a question about the topic of their discussion. Cleopas's counter-question suggested that Jesus had to be the only person in Jerusalem not to know what had gone on. Ironically, only Jesus truly grasps what has transpired.

Downcast, gloomy, sad, the disciples confessed their belief about Jesus (a "Prophet mighty in deed and word before God and all the people") and their dashed hope that he was the Messiah ("the one to redeem Israel").

Cleopas and his companion continued with their catalogue of the happenings, mentioning the discovery of the empty tomb and a report that "some women of our group" had seen "a vision of Angels who said that [Jesus] was alive". Despite verification by some of their group that the facts were as the women had said, for these two travellers the matter was ended. Still, they continued to try to make sense of what had happened.

Jesus then introduced his interlocutors to the Christian manner of reading the Law and the prophets ("beginning with Moses and all the Prophets"), interpreting what had taken place in the Passion narrative and in the early hours of Easter. The key to understanding the Old Testament – the Church continues to argue using Jesus' method – is to perceive that the Scriptures point to suffering and death as God's will for the Messiah ("Was it not necessary?") before he could "enter into his glory".

In the first reading – from the Acts of the Apostles – Peter reads the psalms (part of the third or "Writings" section of the Old Testament) in a Christological manner. Citing Psalm 16 at length, Peter declared that David spoke of Jesus when foretelling that God would not "abandon my soul to Hades or let your Holy One experience corruption".

Further, the first Letter of Peter claims that Christ's suffering and death ("the precious blood of Christ") had been "destined before the foundation of the world" – prior to the existence of Scriptures. However, public revelation of these truths could take place only "at the end of the ages", an era inaugurated by the intervention of God, "who raised [Christ] from the dead and gave him glory".

As the hiking party neared Emmaus, Jesus "walked ahead as if he were going on". Though Jesus began his teaching by reproaching the two disciples for being "foolish" and "slow of heart to believe", they sensed something different – that their hearts had been burning within them "while he was talking to us on the road, while he was opening the Scriptures to us".

Only at table – when "he took bread, blessed and broke it, and gave it to them" – did the disciples recognize Jesus. Suddenly, he vanished from their presence. Though it was late and the journey long, the Emmaus disciples returned to Jerusalem, learning upon arrival of the pivotal appearance to Peter ("The Lord has risen indeed, and he has appeared to Simon!") and then telling their story of how the Lord "had been made known to them in the breaking of the bread".

The Church's celebration of the Eucharist – sharing, as it does, the significance of the Scriptures and Jesus' paschal mystery for the lives of present-day disciples and culminating in the "breaking of the bread" – continues today what Jesus did for a troubled couple on the Emmaus road.

Fourth Sunday of Easter

Jesus Is the Gate for the Sheep

* 1st reading: Acts 2.14a, 36b-41
* Psalm: 23
* 2nd reading: 1 Peter 2.20b-25
* Gospel: John 10.1-10

The Fourth Sunday of Easter is traditionally known as Good Shepherd Sunday and is observed as the World Day of Prayer for Priestly Vocations. The urgency of encouraging those whom Jesus is calling to open themselves to becoming shepherd-priests on the model he offers cannot be underestimated. This intention belongs in Christian prayer not just today, but constantly.

Today's gospel portion from John stops just short of Jesus' declaration that "I am the Good Shepherd" (verses 11, 14). Instead, we find Jesus' description of how shepherds and sheep normally related to one another in Palestine, followed by his application of this teaching to the relationship he shares with his followers.

The extended simile – telling of a shepherd, sheep, a gatekeeper as well as the communication system used between the shepherd and his sheep – contrasts the true shepherd with the false (the "stranger", characterized also as "a thief and a bandit").

The evangelist calls Jesus' teaching a "figure of speech" that "they [the Pharisees with whom Jesus was debating after the healing of the blind man] did not understand". On the surface, Jesus' teaching seems fairly straightforward. Perhaps the Pharisees' incomprehension derived from confusion about how to apply Jesus' statement to the case before them.

For Jesus was implicitly claiming to be the shepherd who fulfilled God's promise of gathering the scattered flock of Israel, as Ezekiel and others had foretold (cf. Ezekiel 34.1-31). The first Letter of Peter described the past behaviour of disciples as "going astray like sheep" and their conversion as returning to Christ, "the shepherd and guardian of your souls".

The issues underlying Jesus' instruction encompass not only the identity of the true shepherd but also the issue of who may rightly be called God's sheep. The man blind from birth showed himself to be one of God's flock by committing himself to Jesus. What of the Pharisees? They appear to have reached a judgment against Jesus. God's verdict, however, will find echoes in the imagery elaborated by Jesus as he continues the discourse.

What may have proven puzzling to Jesus' hearers (and to readers today) is Jesus' double identification of himself as the gate for the sheep ("I am the gate"), a prelude to his double claim to be the Good Shepherd.

After hearing him speak about shepherd and sheep, one might have expected Jesus to state something like "I am the shepherd" (and "you are the sheep"). Instead, we have Jesus' solemn pronouncement ("Very truly, I tell you") that he is the way to salvation ("I am the gate for the sheep .... Whoever enters by me will be saved, and will come in and go out and find pasture"). Jesus says, further, that salvation implies people will "have life, and have it abundantly"). Jesus hints that people know what a gate or door means – for example, escape from prison or an entry point for heaven. This he mysteriously claims to embody!

On its own, the gate metaphor might suggest that Jesus is passive while fulfilling his role as the Way (and the Truth and the Life [cf. John 14.6]). Not so, however, when one sees this reality within the dynamic notion that Jesus "comes" to others as their Messiah. In the gospels, Jesus claimed the title "The Coming One" for himself (cf. Matthew 11.3). And several times Jesus declared his purpose with a phrase that began "the Son of Man has come" – "to give his life as a ransom for many" (Mark 10.45); "to seek and to save the lost" (Luke 19.10).

John's tradition, which spoke of "abundant life", revealed Jesus offering his disciples not time to fill, but a quality of life to be lived fully. This is symbolized beautifully in the "green pastures" and other motifs of comfort mentioned in Psalm 23 ("still waters", "my cup overflows", etc.), which have consoled God's people for three millennia.

Peter's Pentecost discourse shows conversion as being "cut to the heart" and searching for a course of action. Repentance, baptism for the forgiveness of sins and reception of the Holy Spirit are a summary of how the abundant life with Jesus begins. Not recognizing "the voice of strangers" but following Jesus and heeding his voice describe the manner by which one continues to live the abundant life begun in Christian initiation.

Fifth Sunday of Easter

Jesus Returns to the Father

* 1st reading: Acts 6.1-7
* Psalm: 33
* 2nd reading: 1 Peter 2.4-9
* Gospel: John 14.1-12

Last week, Jesus declared that he was the "gate for the sheep", offering them security, pasture and, ultimately, salvation. In today's gospel, Jesus reiterates these truths under different and more personal terms. "I am the way, and the truth, and the life. No one comes to the Father except through me".

These words of Jesus are part of a lengthy farewell discourse that he gave to the disciples in the upper room following the Last Supper (John 13.31–17.26). Jesus addresses his followers in every generation, preparing them for his return to God and the sending of the Holy Spirit as his way of being present to them.

The structure of Jesus' teaching is not strictly logical. Rather, Jesus returns to themes time and again, developing them and adding nuances as he does so. One can detect a pattern in the first part of Jesus' instruction in the four questions put by Peter (13.33), Thomas (14.5), Philip (14.8) and Judah (14.22)—only two of which are in the Gospel reading of today.

Each inquiry deals with Jesus' departure: Peter's question, "Lord, where are you going?" Thomas's assertion and question, "Lord, we do not know where you are going. How can we know the way?" Philip's demand, "Lord, show us the Father", in effect repeats Peter's question, "Where are you going?" Finally, Judah wonders, "Lord, how is it that you will reveal yourself to us, and not to the world?"

Behind all four questions lies the plaintive cry to Jesus, "Why must you leave us?" This appeal echoes the early Christian community's concern about how to sustain the dynamism unleashed by Jesus now that he would be absent from the world in which the Church lived.

ARCHBISHOP TERRENCE PRENDERGAST

Jesus' answer was a call to his disciples to believe in him as they believed in God ("Believe in God, believe also in me" [14.2]).

Jesus' first words in answer to Simon Peter's question were "Where I am going, you cannot follow me now; but you will follow afterward" [13.36]. These words were addressed in the singular, only to Peter, suggesting that at his death Peter would follow Jesus to the Father. As Jesus continued his reply, however, he switched to the plural, speaking to all disciples. "In my Father's house there are many dwelling places. If it were not so, would I have told you that I go to prepare a place for you?" (14.2)

Jesus then made a promise: "And if I go ... I will come again and will take you to myself". Because Jesus did not use eschatological language, it is not clear whether his "coming" refers to Jesus' coming to each individual in the mystery of death or whether it refers to his glorious coming as the Son of Man at the Parousia. In either case, Jesus' purpose in coming ("... so that where I am, there you may be also") is meant to bring consolation to all who believe in him. Here, then, is the basis for Jesus' opening exhortation: "Do not let your hearts be troubled".

Mention of "the Father", whom believers will meet when Jesus leads them to the kingdom, prompts Philip's request that Jesus "show us the Father" and Jesus' rejoinder that "whoever has seen me has seen the Father". Jesus intimated that access to the Father is more than just through one's resurrection on the last day. One has it now by faith.

For faith makes it possible to hear the Father speaking in Jesus' words and to see God at work in the deeds of Jesus. And these works of God, Jesus says, will henceforth be done on earth by the Church once he is absent from the world ("Very truly, I tell you, the one who believes in me will also do the works I do and, in fact, will do greater works than these, because I am going to the Father").

Peter puts Jesus' teaching in other terms, describing the vocation of Christians living in the world as that of letting themselves be built into a "holy priesthood, to offer spiritual sacrifices to God through Jesus Christ".

In the Acts of the Apostles, the dynamism of the early Church is manifest in the Spirit-inspired development of a social assistance program for impoverished widows. The seven "deacons" who served the poor were chosen from among those "full of the Spirit and of wisdom".

Sixth Sunday of Easter

The Holy Spirit, Advocate of Christians

* 1st reading: Acts 8.5-8, 14-17
* Psalm: 66
* 2nd reading: 1 Peter 3.15-18
* Gospel: John 14.15-21

Today's gospel introduces a description of the Holy Spirit that employs the Greek noun *parakletos*. The noun comes from a Greek word meaning "to comfort and console", "to exhort and encourage" or "to appeal to or call upon for help". As such, the noun's meaning would encompass the following range: "one who comforts, exhorts, helps or appeals on one's behalf".

Various modern translations try to encompass these nuances, describing the Holy Spirit as "the Comforter", "the Counsellor" or "the Advocate". Someone hearing John's gospel read in Greek would probably have caught resonances of all these interpretations. Jesus described the Holy Spirit as "*another* Advocate", suggesting that the disciples already possessed an Advocate in the one leaving them – namely, himself.

In the Fourth Gospel, Jesus is never explicitly cited as an Advocate for his disciples. But he is so described in 1 John 2.1 ("we have an advocate with the Father, Jesus Christ the righteous"). This suggests that Jesus' present advocacy on behalf of his followers takes place in heaven. We may also infer that Jesus' advocacy of his disciples

ARCHBISHOP TERRENCE PRENDERGAST

took place during his earthly ministry as well, whenever he helped and strengthened them.

As he took leave of them, Jesus promised his disciples support and encouragement through the Holy Spirit whom the Father would send at his urging ("I will ask the Father, and he will give you another Advocate, to be with you forever"). This Spirit-Advocate would be present in them in a mysterious and hidden way. The world – hostile to Jesus and his way – "neither sees him nor knows him". Jesus' disciples, however, know the Spirit intimately because, as Jesus pledges, "He abides with you, and he will be in you."

Jesus promised not to abandon his disciples ("I will not leave you orphaned"). Rather, he pledged to come to them ("I am coming to you"). But which coming did Jesus mean? Does this refer to the Parousia, to the resurrection or, as some think, to the gift of the Spirit?

While no definitive answer may be asserted without qualification – for Jesus' teaching in John's gospel at times permits several possible ways of being understood – we prefer to think that Jesus refers here to his resurrection. For Jesus spoke of "a little while" (possibly a reference to his death) and said that his disciples would live because of his risen life ("because I live, you also will live").

What is suggested here is that Jesus' "hour" – a mixture of dark suffering and risen glory – inaugurated a new age of intimacy with God ("On that day you will know that I am in my Father, and you in me, and I in you"). This era of the Holy Spirit permits the historical disciples' experience of the risen Lord to become accessible to believers in every age.

The Spirit becomes manifest in the love disciples bear towards one another. In the Spirit, the glorified and risen Jesus comes to believers and moves them towards love ("The one who has my commandments and keeps them is the one who loves me; and the one who loves me will be loved by my Father, and I will love them and reveal myself to them").

Jesus' special teaching about how the Holy Spirit becomes manifest in believers' lives, found only in the Fourth Gospel, appears in four "Paraclete" passages scattered through Jesus' farewell address (cf. John 14.26; 15.26; 16.8-11, 12-15). Perhaps the most significant role of the Holy Spirit is that of dynamically bringing to memory in the lives of Jesus' disciples all that Jesus taught ("the Advocate, the Holy Spirit, whom the Father will send in my name, will teach you everything, and remind you of all that I have said to you" [14.26]).

The reading from Acts recalls that one way the Holy Spirit gets communicated to new believers in the Church is by the apostolic laying on of hands, a gesture signifying the transmission of a blessing to others.

Among the fruits of the Holy Spirit's presence, the first Letter of Peter reminds struggling Christians, is that of helping Jesus' friends to "be ready to make your defence to anyone who demands from you an accounting for the hope that is in you".

The Ascension of the Lord

Christ's Glory

* 1st reading: Acts 1.1-11
* Psalm: 47
* 2nd reading: Ephesians 1.17-23
* Gospel: Matthew 28.16-20

The ascension of Jesus and his entering into God's glory are frequently presupposed in the Scriptures. Still, only Luke describes it. Twice – at the end of his gospel (Luke 24.51) and at the beginning of the Acts of the Apostles (Acts 1.9).

The "ascension" might easily be called Jesus' "assumption". For he is on the receiving end of God's action. The texts in Luke and Acts say, "He was carried up into heaven" and "he was lifted up, and a cloud took him out of their sight". As in all of Jesus' ministry, then, God was active in Jesus' departure from the world.

We might imagine Jesus' glorification after his death as a double-sided coin. The resurrection is the main side of the coin; the ascen-

ARCHBISHOP TERRENCE PRENDERGAST

sion is the other. Saint Paul described it in the letter to the Ephesians: God's mighty power was twice at work in Christ – in raising him from the dead and in making him sit at God's right hand.

The closing verses of Matthew's gospel are consoling in regard to what follows from Christ's ascension. First, Matthew shows that the resurrection did not and does not remove struggles from the lives of disciples. After the resurrection, the Eleven met Jesus on a mountain in Galilee. We are told that they worshipped Jesus, "but some doubted". Even after the resurrection, then, belief can be weak.

Still, Jesus gave the "Great Commission" to such hesitant believers: "Make disciples of all nations ... teaching them to obey everything that I have commanded you". Circumcision had been the sign of entry into Judaism. Now, baptism in the name of the Father, the Son and the Holy Spirit (the Trinitarian formula Christians use in baptismal ceremonies) is the means for entering on the path leading to eternal life.

Jesus' final words are most reassuring. For at his conception, Joseph learned that Mary's child would be *Emmanuel*, "God-with-us". Following his ascension, Jesus remains with his Church: "Remember, I am with you always, to the end of the age".

The "end of the age" means until the end of history when Jesus will return in glory. In other words, Jesus is always with his Church, with those people of "little faith" who cling to his commands as these are interpreted by the apostles' successors, the Pope and bishops.

The hesitation of the Eleven appears in the opening scene of Acts as confusion regarding the kingdom ("Lord, is this the time when you will restore the kingdom to Israel?") Despite all Jesus' instructions to them (even during the forty days after his Resurrection – Acts 1.3), they were still interpreting Jesus' task as the political restoration of David's dynasty. This is the area in which the Holy Spirit would enlighten the apostles after Pentecost.

Jesus reminded his apostles of the mystery of God's designs, which escape human understanding: "It is not for you to know the times or periods that the Father has set by his own authority". Instead, Jesus called them to be witnesses in Jerusalem, in all Judea and Samaria – the areas that had rejected him during his ministry. Spirit-led, they would carry their testimony "to the ends of the earth". In this way Jesus predicted the worldwide mission described in the Acts of the Apostles.

The root meaning of witness (in Greek, *martyros*) is "to bear in mind". Witnessing, then, means remembering and telling about someone or something. The apostles told what they had observed about Jesus. Their devotion to the truth led them to belief and to proclamation of their convictions.

The apostolic witness handed on by the Church concerned facts, not ideas or myths, about Jesus. In every age, the Holy Spirit similarly empowers weak people to go out and, as the apostles did, share the truth about Jesus fearlessly with the world.

The Christian's yearning to witness to Christ becomes a prayer in Ephesians. The Christian asks to experience what God did in Christ's glorification and ascension so that he or she can share it with the world. Christian faith in Jesus' ascension implies hope for what God will do in disciples at the end of their lives as well as at the end of time ("not only in this age but also in the age to come").

Seventh Sunday of Easter[1]

Waiting in Patient Prayer

* 1st reading: Acts 1.12-14
* Psalm: 27
* 2nd reading: 1 Peter 4.13-16
* Gospel: John 17.1-11a

An ancient tradition sees the time between the ascension and Pentecost as a time of prayer for the outpouring of the Holy Spirit on the Church. Between the fortieth day of Easter (Ascension Thursday) and the fiftieth day (Pentecost Sunday) there

---

1 For use in countries and ecclesiastical provinces where the Ascension is celebrated on Thursday.

are nine days, the basis of the Catholic custom of praying a "novena". This is the tradition behind the Novena to the Holy Spirit taking place these days.

In the gospel, we hear the beginning of the "High Priestly Prayer" of Jesus (John 17.1-26). It marks a pivotal point in the dynamic of the Fourth Gospel, bridging the earlier activity and sayings of Jesus – particularly about the coming of the Holy Spirit (14.15-26; 16.4b-15) – as Jesus prepares his disciples for his passion, death and resurrection and for their flight and restoration.

The lengthy prayer of Jesus follows a pattern found in the biblical tradition of an elder's farewell discourse (cf. Jacob in Genesis 49; Moses in Deuteronomy 32; Paul in Acts 20). These conclude with an address to God that those being left behind may be safe, sound and secure for a blessed future.

In this complex prayer of Jesus, found at the Last Supper, a key transition in John's gospel, various issues are addressed in a striking way.

In the first part, eight verses in length, Jesus addresses the heavenly Father seeking his own glorification, for he will soon enter the darkness of his "hour", the passion ("So now, Father, glorify me in your own presence with the glory that I had in your presence before the world existed"). Mention of Jesus' pre-existence as God's Word makes this a prayer of cosmic proportions.

In the second part, extending from verses 9 to 23 (beyond the limits of today's gospel reading, which ends at verse 11), Jesus prays for the community of faith in every age. Significant pronouncements are made that take Jesus and his disciples beyond the constraints of time and space:

- though Jesus is about to take up his cross and go to Golgotha to die, he says, "now I am no longer in the world, but they are in the world, and I am coming to you" (v. 11);

- Jesus speaks as if persecution has already broken out against the disciples, though they have not yet been scattered or reconstituted, nor have they carried out their ministry of witnessing to him: "the world has hated them because they do not belong to the world, just as I do not belong to the world" (v. 14);

- Jesus speaks as if they are already glorified by the gift of the Holy Spirit: "the glory that you have given me I have given them, so that they may be one, as we are one" (v. 22).

Finally, in verses 24 to 26, our Lord prays for the eschatological union of the Father, the Son and all believers, reiterating – with variations – the first great petition of his prayer: "Father, I desire that those also, whom you have given me, may be with me where I am, to see my glory, which you have given me because you loved me before the foundation of the world" (v. 24).

Clearly there is much in this prayer that can be understood by disciples only when they prayerfully enter into it in a contemplative way themselves.

In the passage from Acts, giving time to prayer characterizes the disciples of Jesus, who gather in the Upper Room where Jesus had celebrated the Last Supper with them. They are the Eleven, Mary the Mother of Jesus and other relatives ("his brothers") and "certain women" (Luke 8.1-3; 24.1-11; cf. also John 4, 11), about 120 persons (Acts 1.15) or, in Jewish understanding, the nucleus of a new community of believers.

Under Peter's guidance, the assembled community explores the scriptural basis of Judas Iscariot's defection (Acts 1.15-20). Then they resolve to find a substitute to reconstitute the apostles as the Twelve (1.21-26). After prayer seeking guidance from above, the lot falls to Matthias, after which the disciples continue to patiently await the coming of the Holy Spirit promised by Jesus (cf. Luke 24.49; Acts 1.8).

The passage from the first Letter of Peter echoes the linking of prayer, suffering and glory in Jesus' intercession before the Father for his followers through the ages. Peter underlines the truth that suffering is an inescapable part of the life of Christ's disciples. For such suffering, he says, shares in the suffering of Christ himself and carries with it the promise of final glory.

Pentecost Sunday

All Christians Share the Spirit of Jesus

* 1st reading: Acts 2.1-11
* Psalm: 104
* 2nd reading: 1 Corinthians 12.3b-7, 12-13
* Gospel: John 20.19-23

Some years ago, during a posting in Saskatchewan, I shared the prairie-dweller's experience of the wind. Cool in the summer, gentle in autumn, biting in the winter and fresh during springtime, the wind was never seen but almost always felt.

Christian experience of the Holy Spirit requires becoming attuned to the Spirit's presence, discerning where the Spirit is leading. Perhaps members of the Church need to make wide-open spaces in their hearts so that the Spirit can enter and renew daily life ("Come, Holy Spirit, fill the hearts of your faithful; and kindle in them the fire of your love").

To someone familiar with the Old Testament, Luke's account of Pentecost Day would evoke the giving of the Torah (law) to Moses on Mount Sinai, suggesting as well a reversal of the Tower of Babel story. Later, Peter would explain that the prophecy of Joel had been fulfilled in the outpouring of the Holy Spirit that the bystanders had witnessed.

The "Feast of Weeks" – held on the fiftieth day of the spring harvest (*Pentekostes*, in Greek) – marked the close of Israel's celebration of God's many blessings. Israel thanked God for the bounty of the fields and for the greater bounty of God's love in choosing a covenant people. God's election of Israel at Sinai, then, came to be linked with Pentecost, just as the Exodus had been with Passover.

At Pentecost, Israel praised God's self-revelation on Sinai in "fire", "wind" and – according to first-century rabbinic writings – in "tongues". Luke described the Pentecost following Jesus' resurrection and ascension as God's newest self-manifestation. Through the Holy Spirit, who carries on Jesus' ministry both to the ends of the earth and to all its peoples, God had become present in the world in a marvellously new way.

In a catalogue of places sweeping from east to west (from Parthia to Rome), Luke proclaimed that the Spirit of God was moving over the face of the world, unifying one and all in praise of God. Pentecost appears as a new beginning for humanity's relationship with God. As the rest of the Acts of the Apostles shows, God's marvels had only just begun.

Chapters twelve to fourteen of the first Letter to the Corinthians are a wonderful treatise on the way the Holy Spirit guides and directs the Church, the Body of Christ. Paul began his presentation by noting that, when they had been unbelievers, the Corinthians were pushed by "spirits" in a variety of directions leading nowhere. People seem ready to follow such spirits every which way in this world.

Paul said that the True and Holy Spirit may be recognized by the positive direction given to believers. Also Jesus' Spirit causes them to confess with their lips and their lives that "Jesus is Lord". Whatever one's special gift (and there is a great variety of gifts), Paul stresses that these have been given to the individual believers by "the [one and] same Spirit". No one can claim anything he or she has, except as a gift from "the same God who activates all of them in everyone".

It seems that the Corinthians, after their initial enthusiasm at having received spiritual gifts that could be used in service to the community, began wrangling about which gift (and which person, therefore) was the most important. The gifts that God had intended to foster the unity of the Body of Christ became, instead, an occasion of its being torn apart. How often in every age this has been the experience of the Church! What began with hopeful optimism later collapses in squabbling and acrimony among Christians ....

Still, Paul never became discouraged, no matter how petty the arguments among the disciples of Jesus. He knew that it was God who had begun the good work among the Corinthians, and

ARCHBISHOP TERRENCE PRENDERGAST

God would faithfully see them through blameless to the end (cf. 1 Corinthians 1.4-9).

Here, Paul takes the same optimistic tack, urging his converts and their friends to recall that they were all baptized into one body – Christ's – and through that baptism all were given a share of the one Spirit of Jesus ("and we were all made to drink of one Spirit").

The Solemnity of the Most Holy Trinity

"God So Loved the World"

* 1st reading: Exodus 34.4b-6, 8-9
* Responsorial canticle: Daniel 3
* 2nd reading: 2 Corinthians 13.11-13
* Gospel: John 3.16-18

The solemnity of the Most Holy Trinity issued from the Christological and Trinitarian controversies of the fourth and fifth centuries. By the ninth century, a votive Mass of the Trinity had gained in popularity. Monasteries observed this feast on the Sunday after Pentecost before it was extended to the universal Church in 1334.

Trinity Sunday does not recall a specific saving action of God. Rather, it reminds Christians of their doctrinal belief, professing that God, Christ and the Spirit are equally responsible for salvation.

Christians are neither "tri-theists" (believing in three gods) nor "modalists" (believing that Father, Son and Spirit are simply different appearances taken on by God in various stages of history). Rather, for orthodox (right-believing) Christians there is only the One God, revealed in salvation history and existing as the Trinity, a community of three Divine Persons.

In the Preface for this feast, God the Father is praised: "We joyfully proclaim our faith in the mystery of your Godhead. You have revealed your glory as the glory also of your Son and of the Holy

Spirit: three Persons equal in majesty, undivided in splendour, yet one Lord, one God, ever to be adored in your everlasting glory".

Nowhere is the dogma of the Trinity explicitly stated in the Scriptures in the way that the Church formulated it at the major Councils. However, the nucleus of the doctrine is present allusively in formulas, greetings and prayers. Paul made use of one such formulation to conclude his Second Letter to the Corinthians ("the grace of the Lord Jesus Christ, the love of God, and the communion of the Holy Spirit be with all of you").

Theologians who research about the Trinity distinguish between the "immanent" Trinity (the inner life shared by the Persons of the Godhead) and the "economic" Trinity (the divine nature as it is revealed through God's saving acts in history).

In fact, most of what we can know of God's nature must derive from what we may postulate from observations made about God's actions towards humanity and the rest of creation. These are supplemented by the revelation Jesus has given – mainly in John's Gospel – of his relationships with the Father and the Holy Spirit, as well as in occasional remarks Jesus makes in the synoptic gospels.

Today's reading from Exodus reflects on God's nature after a crisis in salvation history. God had rescued Israel from bondage in Egypt and begun the process of forming them into a holy people, offering them the tablets of the covenant to guide their life. Their answer had been rebellion and idolatry while Moses was on the mountain receiving the revelation.

What was God to do? The answer was to begin again with new tablets. But God did more, declaring to Moses the divine characteristics implicit in his Name. These characteristics give believers insights about God's nature. God's nature may be known by means of the seven attributes God reveals:

God is "merciful" (a term related to the word for "womb" and suggesting God's womb-like mother-love); "gracious" (having a completely gratuitous disposition, giving without merit); "slow to anger" (the Hebrew means literally "with a long nostril" that allows the divine wrath to cool before it can destroy); "abounding in steadfast

ARCHBISHOP TERRENCE PRENDERGAST

love" (God has a great capacity to be loyal, putting up with a great deal, even when Israel reneges); "faithfulness" (God is completely reliable); "keeping steadfast love" (to the thousandth generation); and "forgiving" (literally meaning that God removes the burden of sin and violations of the covenant).

In the gospel, Jesus said that what had been revealed of God in the past found a new manifestation in his having been sent from the Father: "God so loved the world that he gave his only-begotten Son, so that everyone who believes in him may not perish but may have eternal life".

The way to participate in God's saving plan is by faith. Those who do not believe condemn themselves to live outside of this rich divine life that God yearns to share with creatures. From God's very nature comes not condemnation but salvation ("God did not send the Son into the world to condemn the world, but in order that the world might be saved through him").

The Solemnity of the Most Holy Body and Blood of Christ

Feeding on the Bread of Life

* 1st reading: Deuteronomy 8.2-3, 14-16
* Psalm: 147
* 2nd reading: 1 Corinthians 10.16-17
* Gospel: John 6.51-59

One of the puzzling aspects of the Fourth Gospel is why John gives no account of the Eucharist when he tells about the Last Supper. In its place we read the story of Jesus washing his disciples' feet. As a sign of his loving the disciples "to the end", Jesus' gesture foretold both his laying down his life on the cross and his taking it up again in the resurrection. In commanding his disciples to do as he had done – serving one another selflessly – Jesus shared his outlook as he gave his life in obedience to the Father's will.

In compensation for his lack of reference to the institution of the Eucharist, John reports a lengthy address given by Jesus in the Capernaum synagogue shortly after the miracle of the multiplication of the loaves (John 6.1-15). The "Bread of Life" discourse (John 6.26-59) is an extended reflection by Jesus on a text found in Psalm 78.24 ("He gave them the grain of heaven [to eat]").

Jesus linked his teaching with the events of the Exodus, when God daily fed the people with manna. Surprisingly, God's provident care evoked only grumbling from the people, as Jesus' teaching and claims to be the "true bread from heaven" did among his contemporaries.

Jesus also tied his instruction on the Bread of Life to the prophetic tradition about the word of God, which nourishes and confronts God's people. Jesus' teaching feeds God's people and challenges them to be obedient to God's ways. At the climax of his dialogue, Jesus identified himself with God's heavenly food ("I am the Bread of Life").

Jesus' closing words evoke images of his self-offering on the cross ("the bread that I will give for the life of the world is my flesh"). And the words that Jesus speaks about eating his flesh and drinking his blood suggest a parallel to the Words of Institution found in the synoptic gospels ("Take, eat … this is my body"; "Take and drink … this is my blood…").

Still, the fact that Jesus did not link bread and wine and referred to his "flesh" rather than his "body" has led some interpreters and Protestant churches (notably Evangelicals) to deny that Jesus refers to the Eucharist. They see, instead, a continuation of Jesus' insistence that his disciples feed on his teaching, moving them to follow Christ to martyrdom as Jesus had gone obediently to his death.

Catholic Christians see in the flow of Jesus' teaching in the Bread of Life discourse the same development that takes place at Mass. The Christ who preaches his word in the Scriptures in the first part of the liturgy gives himself to his people in the Eucharistic meal.

Jesus challenges each disciple to believe, offering him or her eternal life now ("Whoever eats my flesh and drinks my blood has eternal life"). This eternal life will come to full flower in the resurrection at the end of time ("and I will raise them up on the last day").

Between the act of believing in Jesus and the day of resurrection, believers are sustained by both Jesus' teaching and his presence in the Eucharist ("Whoever eats my flesh and drinks my blood abides in me, and I in them").

In his first Letter to the Corinthians, Paul speaks of the social dimension of the Eucharist. The individual believer becomes one with Christ in the Eucharist. Paul adds that, through communion with Christ, he or she also enters into union with all those who share the "one bread" of Christ's body ("we who are many are one body, for we all partake of the one bread").

Much as the Johannine tradition offers profound insights into Jesus' teaching, the Book of Deuteronomy reflects on the traditions found in Exodus and Numbers and presents them in a new way. Moses asked the people to look back and see what God had been doing – namely, allowing people to experience hunger so they could understand "that one does not live by bread alone, but by every word that comes from the mouth of the Lord". Christians might add "and by every word that comes from the mouth of the Lord Jesus" who, they believe, is the "bread that came down from heaven".

Tenth Sunday in Ordinary Time

"I Desire Mercy, Not Sacrifice"

* 1st reading: Hosea 6.3-6
* Psalm: 50
* 2nd reading: Romans 4.18-25
* Gospel: Matthew 9.9-13

In today's gospel, a recurring theme is God's mercy, which – along with justice and faith – is one of the "weightier matters of the law" (Matthew 23.23).

Matthew depicts Jesus as the teacher whose instruction fulfills the teaching of the great lawgiver Moses and the message of the prophets. Jesus cites a text from the prophet Hosea (6.6) – in which God argues, "I desire steadfast love and not sacrifice" – to justify his reaching out to sinners, like Matthew the tax collector, as a key to his ministry.

The concept translated by "steadfast love" in Hosea and "mercy" in the gospel interprets the Hebrew term *chesed*. This word describes the spirit of covenantal fellowship that ought to exist between parties who have made a binding agreement.

Chesed's "fundamental meaning is loyalty and faithfulness to a covenant. Nevertheless, the term does have a variety of other meanings, as we see from our modern translations: love (used frequently in the liturgy), grace, goodness, loving-kindness. These translations emphasize the emotional aspect, the interior disposition of the *chesed*; however, we must not lose sight of the concrete meaning of the term as an act of faithfulness to a covenant that derives from a situation of solidarity between the one who is faithful and the recipient of the faithfulness" (Jean-Pierre Prevost, *A Short Dictionary of the Psalms*, p. 42).

The middle of Hosea (5.8–8.14) presents a series of oracular statements uttered by Hosea on God's behalf. They address internal and external issues of the northern kingdom (Ephraim), which was in rebellion against God. God's people are flighty and inconstant ("Your love is like a morning cloud, like the dew that goes away early"). References to Judah, the southern kingdom, show that it, too, was unfaithful.

God said that his people continually acted contrary to the Torah, which was given to help them live in covenant faithfulness, *chesed*. So God promised a variety of means to draw Israel back in love: rending and striking down, healing and building up (5.15–6.3). God's goal was the people's repentance, getting them to turn back so they could be restored to their former glory, to delight in being God's chosen ones.

In this context God declared dissatisfaction with sacrifices offered by worshippers whose hearts belied their actions. Those offering sacrifice in this way were dishonest, for their conduct blatantly contradicted the demands of the covenant.

Only if their attitude were imbued with *chesed* – covenantal fidelity, goodness and mercy – could their sacrifices become acceptable to God. To effect such a conversion, God asserted, "I desire steadfast love [mercy, kindness, goodness] more than [empty] sacrifice".

The importance of this "mercy" text for Matthew's portrait of Jesus may be gauged from the fact that it is quoted again in Jesus' controversy with the Pharisees over Sabbath observances (Matthew 12.7). There Jesus justified his abrogation of a stipulation of the law by claiming that he was the final arbitrator of God's will expressed in Torah and Sabbath commandments ("the Son of Man is lord of the Sabbath").

Jesus' mission is based on mercy, not merit. In this perspective there is no one so base – not even the tax collector, despised in his time for collaborating with the Roman occupying force – as to be outside Jesus' concern and call.

Jesus had reached out to Matthew, one of the dregs of society, and established him as a fellow worker in proclaiming the kingdom.

Matthew's banquet, offered in gratitude, became a model representing the gospel joy that comes into a person's life after surrendering to Jesus' call. The community around Jesus – the church in every age – continues to call sinners to accept the healing, which Jesus liberally offers.

Jesus described himself as the "Divine Physician", ready to heal all broken by sin and the hurts of life ("those who are well have no need of a physician, but those who are sick").

Only those who feel they have no need of forgiveness and healing exclude themselves from his concern: "I have come to call not the righteous but sinners".

Eleventh Sunday in Ordinary Time

Jesus Sends His Disciples on Mission

* 1st reading: Exodus 19.1-6a
* Psalm: 100
* 2nd reading: Romans 5.6-11
* Gospel: Matthew 9.36–10.8

The nineteenth chapter of the Book of Exodus marked the beginning of a new era in God's relationship with Israel. After rescuing Israel from bondage in Egypt, God would communicate the terms of his covenant with the people over a period of eleven months at Mount Sinai. This period of intimacy between God and Israel was so pivotal that the rest of the book of Exodus, along with all of Leviticus and the first part of the book of Numbers, takes place at God's mountain.

The purpose of the sojourn at Sinai was to instil in the Israelites the notion that they were God's "treasured possession out of all the peoples". God lays claim to all the world ("the whole earth is mine") and gives Israel a special vocation, that of being for God "a priestly kingdom and a holy nation".

God's people are to be priests, serving rather than ruling over others, acting as intermediaries – the way priests do – to bring the nations of the earth to God. Peter sees the Church continuing this special mission of Israel: "You are a chosen race, a royal priesthood, a holy nation, God's own people, in order that you may proclaim the mighty acts of him who called you out of darkness into his marvellous light" (1 Peter 2.9).

With rare exceptions, the public ministry of Jesus was directed "to the lost sheep of the house of Israel". In Matthew's account, only after the resurrection did Jesus send the Eleven to evangelize the nations of the world ("Go ... make disciples of all nations, baptizing

ARCHBISHOP TERRENCE PRENDERGAST

them ... and teaching them to obey everything that I have commanded you"). During their participation in Jesus' ministry from a
base in Galilee, the twelve disciples were similarly limited in their
outreach ("Go nowhere among the Gentiles, and enter no town of
the Samaritans").

In teaching and healing the crowds who flocked to him, Jesus
became aware of their plight ("they were harassed and helpless, like
sheep without a shepherd"). Jesus' first observation to the disciples
was that the situation called for prayer to God so that others might
be associated with him ("the harvest is plentiful, but the labourers
are few; therefore ask the Lord of the harvest to send out labourers
into his harvest").

Jesus deputed twelve disciples to carry out his two-fold ministry
of healing ("authority over unclean spirits, to cast them out, and to
cure every disease and every sickness") and teaching ("As you go, proclaim the good news, 'The kingdom of heaven has come near'").

All that Jesus had been seen to do in Matthew 8–9 – curing the
sick, raising the dead, cleansing lepers and casting out demons – the
disciples were to do. And all of this they were to do freely, without thinking of recompense ("You received without payment; give
without payment").

The evangelist Matthew has given order and structure to the
mission-sending discourse of Jesus, even pairing the names of the
disciples two by two (for example, "Philip and Bartholomew; Thomas
and Matthew the tax collector").

Matthew has expanded several shorter mission addresses of Jesus
(cf. Mark 6.7-11 and Luke 10.2-12) into an extended presentation
that calls disciples in every age to courageous confession of faith in
him and lays out the cost of being a disciple (Matthew 10.24-33 and
34-39), the gospel readings for the next two Sundays.

In this way, Matthew illustrates the continuity between the words
Jesus spoke in the past to his disciples in Galilee and those he now
speaks to the Church in every age through his presence in the Church
("Remember, I am with you always, to the end of the age").

Continuity in God's saving plan is also the theme of Paul's letter to the Romans. Paul wants the Romans – and believers of every age who worry about the future – to see that the salvation God's "love for us" has won through the death of Christ "while we still were sinners" will be brought to its completion in the future ("much more surely then ... will we be saved through [Christ] from the wrath of God").

Far from fearing God, then, Christians delight in being near to God through their relationship with Jesus ("we even boast in God through our Lord Jesus Christ").

Twelfth Sunday in Ordinary Time

Jesus Urges His Disciples, "Have No Fear"

* 1st reading: Jeremiah 20.10-13
* Psalm: 69
* 2nd reading: Romans 5.12-15
* Gospel: Matthew 10.26-33

When Jesus delivered the Sermon on the Mount, the disciples became aware of the challenges they faced to live in accord with his teaching. At that point – the centre of his address – Jesus eased their burden by encouraging them three times "do not worry about your life ..., about tomorrow" (Matthew 6.25, 31, 34). Jesus assured them that God cares for all his children, lavishing them with love and watching over them.

In today's gospel reading, which is the mid-point of Jesus' mission-sending discourse, we find a similar three-fold invitation from Jesus to have no fear (Matthew 10.26, 28, 31).

As in the Sermon on the Mount, these words of consolation come after rather sobering statements by Jesus that his disciples would be subject to the same lot he faced: persecution, rejection, even betrayal

ARCHBISHOP TERRENCE PRENDERGAST

by members of one's own family (10.16-25). For "a disciple is not above the teacher" (10.24).

The disciple of Jesus knows he or she need not fear because God is the sovereign Lord. Whatever befalls them must – in some way – be in keeping with God's will. For life on this earth is not what ultimately matters. What truly counts is not the suffering endured now but one's future in the world to come. The only true "fear" is reverence directed to God "who can destroy both soul and body in hell" of any who choose to live outside God's pattern for humans.

Jesus' teaching, then, addresses the issue of "providence" – the benevolent ordering of all the events of history. For believers, nothing comes about by chance. Christians cannot see or understand how, yet do believe that there is a divine plan to the universe. In God, there is a purpose for everything, even if we do not know what it is.

As in the ancient world, people today strive to understand life in the cosmos and to live in harmony with it. For some, this takes on a form of "fatalism" – all has been determined. One cannot do anything to shape destiny. People become passive about their future, doing nothing.

Others are more pro-active. In the past, people read the stars or the entrails of animals to find out what the future held; today many people consult fortune tellers or read their horoscope in the morning paper. Some New Age techniques speak to this desire for harmony with the universe that people feel in our day.

Jesus offers a different set of convictions, seeing providence as God's ordering of even the smallest aspects of human life. In today's gospel, Jesus reveals the Father as One who watches over the birds of the air and knows how many hairs are on each human head. However difficult his teaching may appear, Jesus assures his followers that the Father cares for each creature.

Poor people bought sparrows in bundles of ten in the market-place; sparrows were also hunted and killed. For Jesus, none of this happens apart from the knowledge, power and love of God. Jesus does not explain the mystery. He only invites people to live it, trusting God: "You are of more value than many sparrows".

Jeremiah and Paul struggled to express the mystery of living in light of God's care for them and for the world. At a particularly trying moment in his prophetic career, Jeremiah lamented that he had gotten involved in God's designs: "O Lord, you have enticed me, and I was enticed". He thought it would be delightful to be God's servant, but found himself a "laughingstock" instead. Still, Jeremiah was convinced God would vindicate him, and he rejoiced: "Sing to the Lord; praise the Lord! For he has delivered the life of the needy from the hands of evildoers".

Paul pondered the way in which humanity had become embroiled in the sin of Adam, which brought death into the world ("sin came into the world through one man, and death come through sin, so death spread to all people because all have sinned").

God's reply to this state was to send Jesus to undo sin's grip by his death on the cross. In a paradoxical reply to humanity's plight, God has caused a renewed divine–human friendship ("the grace" and "the free gift") to become more widespread than sin's dominion ever was.

God's provident care knows no bounds.

The Nativity of Saint John the Baptist – June 24

"The Lord Called Me Before I Was Born"

* 1st reading: Isaiah 49.1-6
* Psalm: 139
* 2nd reading: Acts 13.22-26
* Gospel: Luke 1.57-66, 80

During a historic visit to Damascus, Pope John Paul II noted that Syria was dear to Christians because "here our religion has known vital moments of its growth and doctrinal development, and here are found Christian communities which have

ARCHBISHOP TERRENCE PRENDERGAST

lived in peace and harmony with their Muslim neighbours for many centuries".

The Holy Father spoke during a visit to the great Umayyad Mosque, where the skull of St. John the Baptist is venerated. He observed that John is revered not only by Christians, but also by followers of Muhammad.

"We are meeting close to what both Christians and Muslims regard as the tomb of John the Baptist, known as *Yahya* in the Muslim tradition. The son of Zechariah is a figure of prime importance in the history of Christianity, for he was the Precursor who prepared the way for Christ.

"John's life, wholly dedicated to God, was crowned by martyrdom. May his witness enlighten all who venerate his memory here, so that they – and we too – may understand that life's great task is to seek God's truth and justice."

John's prophetic call to serve both Israel and the nations lay hidden within the designs of God. The text from Isaiah offers the background to the Gospel, intimating that God's call was issued before John's birth, as he was being carried in the womb of Elizabeth ("The Lord called me before I was born, while I was in my mother's womb he named me"). This motif is echoed by the psalm ("My frame was not hidden from you, when I was being made in secret").

The majority of Israelite names, like ancient Semitic names in general, had readily understandable meanings. Parents consciously chose such names, which could be translated into sentences, to describe the identity of, or aspirations they had for, their child. The name "Zechariah" means "The Lord remembers", while "John" means "God has been gracious".

John's name was assigned him by the angel Gabriel when Zechariah was told that his wife would conceive and bear a son in her old age. Though Zechariah had been rendered mute for his momentary unbelief, Elizabeth in a wondrous manner had arrived at the divinely appointed name. She insisted on naming her son John.

John's birth is mentioned only cursorily so that attention may be given to the drama of his naming and the end of Zechariah's speechlessness. When Zechariah wrote "his name is John", people were amazed, Zechariah's tongue was loosed and he began praising God, uttering the *Benedictus* (Luke 1.68-79), which the Church prays at Lauds every morning.

The second of the "Servant Songs" of Isaiah (and the others found in 42.1-4; 50.4-9; 52.13–53.12) originally referred to an Israelite spiritual leader of the sixth century BC. Still, it finds resonances in the ministry of Jesus (it evokes the passion of Jesus in Holy Week) and in the career of John.

The Baptist's words were like a sharpened arrow, piercing to the heart believers of his time. As with the "suffering servant", John's labours must have seemed to him emptiness and frustration ("I have laboured in vain, I have spent my strength for nothing and vanity"). But the reading from Isaiah fosters the notion that God reassured John, promising that "I will give you as a light to the nations, that my salvation may reach to the end of the earth".

In the passage from Acts, Peter described the closing of John's preaching career as a selfless one, his humility leading him to speak thus about Jesus. "What do you suppose that I am? I am not he. No, but one is coming after me; I am not worthy to untie the thong of the sandals on his feet".

Around the time of the winter solstice – December 25 – when the course of the sun begins to rise in the northern hemisphere, the Church celebrates the birth of Christ, the shining sun born from on high and the true light of the world; in the same way, at the summer solstice – June 24 – when the course of the sun begins to decline, the Christian community recalls the birth of John the Baptist, who, though not himself the light, bore witness to the light (cf. John 1.6-9).

John himself testified, "he must increase, but I must decrease" (John 3.30), a saying that the Church's liturgy has applied to the location of these feasts in the solar calendar.

Thirteenth Sunday in Ordinary Time

Welcoming Jesus and Newness of Life

* 1st reading: 2 Kings 4.8-12a, 14-16
* Psalm: 89
* 2nd reading: Romans 6.3-4, 8-11
* Gospel: Matthew 10.37-42

One might have expected the conclusion to Jesus' mission address to promise great success and an abundant harvest. Instead, Jesus speaks of the cross ("whoever does not take up their cross and follow me is not worthy of me"). It is a very sobering message. Jesus repeats its core thrust in several different forms. "Whosoever finds their life" [in this world because they dissociate themselves from me] "will lose it, and whosoever loses their life for my sake" [by embracing my way of life] "will find it".

One of the most sacrosanct values of the Mediterranean world in which Jesus and the disciples lived was the family. Jesus did not attack the family as such. But he did note that, if family ties in any way become a hindrance to discipleship, they must be broken. "Whoever loves father or mother more than me is not worthy of me; and whoever loves son or daughter more than me is not worthy of me".

While the authenticity of many individual sayings of Jesus is debated (did Jesus actually say *that?*), these radically counter-cultural declarations are almost universally attributed to him. Implicit in them is the kind of demand that only God can make, pointing to Jesus' unique role in mediating God's will.

The closing verses of Jesus' mission-sending speech recognize that not all disciples can go out on mission. Yet all have a role in supporting the mission by receiving missionaries and supporting their function in the life of the Church. For in receiving one sent by Jesus on mission, the Church receives Jesus and even the Father who sent him. "Whoever welcomes you welcomes me, and whoever welcomes me welcomes the one who sent me".

No one who shows such hospitality to Jesus' emissaries will go unrewarded. "Whoever welcomes a prophet in the name of a prophet will receive a prophet's reward; and whoever welcomes a righteous person in the name of a righteous person will receive the reward of the righteous". (The Semitic phrase "in the name of" means "because someone is".)

Even the gift of a cup of cold water will be rewarded. "Whoever gives even a cup of cold water to one of the little ones [probably a reference to Christian missionaries] in the name of a disciple – truly I tell you that person will not lose their reward". Every disciple, even if he or she cannot be engaged directly in the missionary enterprise, has a role to play in the Church's mission by supporting the heralds of the gospel. Jesus' mission address, then, is for all Christians.

The story of Elisha's meeting with the wealthy, though childless, woman of Shunem illustrates how God has always rewarded generosity to those engaged in the divine mission. She and her husband are rewarded with the promise of a new life ("you shall embrace a son"). This is the child they longed for but dared not expect, as her startled reply to the prophet—not included in the lectionary passage—reveals ("No, my lord, O man of God; do not deceive your servant" [4.16]).

The New Testament uses a number of images to describe baptism, the reception of new life in Christ. In John 3.1-15, the image is one of "new birth"; the new Christian begins a new life of organic growth. Colossians 2.11-15 employs the metaphor of "circumcision", hinting that the one baptized "strips off" fleshly desires and actions. The first Letter of Peter recalls the story of Noah and the Flood to communicate that the waters of baptism save believers from the death of sin.

In Romans, Paul speaks of the disciple being "baptized into Christ Jesus", hinting at the "incorporation" or personal union of Christians with a living person, the Risen Lord. This fits in with Paul's notion that, together, Christians form the Body of Christ.

This view reveals the Church as a relationship that is cosmic in scope. In Christ, Christians are one with believers throughout the world, and the Church is more than a collection of individuals with a common purpose. Sharing in Christ's death to sin and resurrection to new life, the Christian is "alive to God in Christ Jesus" and lives "in newness of life".

Solemnity of Saints Peter and Paul, Apostles – June 29

"Set Free from All My Fears"

* 1st reading: Acts 12.1-11
* Psalm: 34
* 2nd reading: 2 Timothy 4.6-8, 17-18
* Gospel: Matthew 16.13-19

When Halifax, Nova Scotia, was established in 1749, the first established (Anglican) Church was dedicated to Paul, the hero of the Protestant Reformation. Iconography depicts him holding a sword, representing the power of the word of God to set people free.

Some years later, in 1784, Roman Catholics gained civic freedoms in this British colony. They built a church and chose as their patron St. Peter. In iconography, he is depicted holding a set of keys; he is popularly described as the first pope. Today's gospel account of Jesus' commission at Caesarea Philippi, giving Peter the "power of the keys", figures prominently in Catholic thought.

In considering these two heroes of the early Church, one might be tempted to compare and contrast these two apostles and the symbols – keys and sword – that represent them.

However, each of the symbols has multiple meanings. For keys release as well as bind; and while a sword cuts cords that bind, it can also represent the power to restrain or limit. Indeed, the freedom of the gospel – since it is energized by God's power – also binds a person to God's way.

And so the liturgy appropriately chooses to link the great apostles Peter and Paul, each of whom suffered martyrdom, in order to give praise to God whose instruments to spread the gospel they were.

The Preface for today's solemnity thanks God for them both: "Peter, our leader in the faith, and Paul, its fearless preacher. Peter raised up the Church from the faithful flock of Israel. Paul brought your call to the nations and became the teacher of the world. Each in his chosen way gathered into unity the one family of Christ. Both shared a martyr's death and are praised throughout the world".

Peter and Paul are also recognized as the founders of the Church at Rome.

Peter, after guiding and defending the early Church in Jerusalem, is depicted in the Acts of the apostles as a missionary (9.32-42) and arbiter of conflict (15.7-11). He had a vision of foods descending from heaven with the explanation that the former rules of clean (kosher) and unclean (non-kosher) foods no longer applied to Jesus' followers; this also permitted the admission of Gentiles, represented by Cornelius and his household, into the Church (10.1–11.18).

Today's first reading mentions Peter's imprisonment and miraculous escape – divine intervention in his favour – which led to his flight from Jerusalem. Persecution of the Church meant the death of James and Peter's mistreatment at the hands of Herod Agrippa I, a king whose rule was characterized by violence and caprice, underlined by the account of Peter's death (Acts 12.22-24).

The angel of the Lord's rescue of Peter seemed to him at the time like a dream, but it was a manifestation in his life of the Psalmist's experience of God's saving power. This point is captured well by the psalm refrain, "The Lord set me free from all my fears".

Peter subsequently travelled to Antioch, where he and Paul ate together (cf. Galatians 2.11), may have visited Corinth (cf. 1 Corinthians 9.5) and eventually came to Rome. Clement described Peter's trials in Rome, and Eusebius in his *Ecclesiastical History* reports an ancient tradition of Peter's crucifixion upside down near the location of the Vatican Basilica, sometime between the years 52 and 67.

Paul's testament also spoke confidently of divine assistance – received and to come – in the crises of his apostolic ministry. "The Lord stood by me and gave me strength … I was rescued from the lion's mouth … The Lord will rescue me from every evil attack and save me for his heavenly kingdom".

Paul compares his imminent death to the "libation", an offering of wine poured out on top of a sacrifice to accompany and complete it. Sometimes called the "blood of the grape", the libation represented Paul's self-offering to God in death.

Paul attested his cooperation with God's grace ("I have fought the good fight, I have finished the race, I have kept the faith"). Now all the initiative lay in God's hands, and in this fact Paul hoped: "there is reserved for me the crown of righteousness", the victor's crown reserved for every disciple who longs "for [Jesus'] appearing".

An ancient tradition holds that Paul died beheaded on the Ostian Way, five kilometres from Rome, near the Basilica constructed over his tomb.

Fourteenth Sunday in Ordinary Time

Taking on the "Yoke" of Jesus

* 1st reading: Zechariah 9.9-10
* Psalm: 145
* 2nd reading: Romans 8.9, 11-13
* Gospel: Matthew 11.25-30

Alexander the Great's meteoric conquests stirred in the prophet known as Second Zechariah (the author of chapters 9 to 14, written sometime between 332 and 200 BC) faith in what God would do in the end times. God's intention, this prophet believed, was to raise up a ruler in the Davidic line, anointing him to carry out a universal mission of peace and reconciliation.

This future ruler's triumph would come about only at great cost. The anticipated good shepherd would have to undergo much suffering. Indeed, the whole people of God would experience deep purification before his divinely ordained rule could begin. Paradoxically, this mighty king would be poor and committed to peace ("humble and riding on a donkey") rather than to war (riding on a horse).

The prophet foresaw the whole civilized world, from the Mediterranean to the Persian Gulf, as the arena over which the coming Messiah would hold sway ("he shall command peace to the nations; his dominion shall be from sea to sea").

Matthew's gospel cited this text (joined with Isaiah 62.11) as fulfilled in Jesus' messianic entry into Jerusalem (cf. Matthew 21.4). Moreover, the theme of the gentle rule of the messiah is aptly embodied by Jesus' words in today's gospel ("my yoke is easy, and my burden is light").

These consoling verses conclude a chapter in which John the Baptist had wondered whether Jesus truly was the one "who is to come" whom he had proclaimed (Matthew 11.1-15); Jesus' Galilean contemporaries found fault with both John and him (11.16-19); and the cities of Capernaum, Chorazin and Bethsaida refused to repent after hearing his message (11.20-24).

Faced with such unbelief, Jesus spoke of the special relationship he shared with the Father ("no one knows the Son except the Father, and no one knows the Father except the Son and anyone to whom the Son chooses to reveal him"). In the face of resistance, Jesus praises the Father, knowing that his will is being worked out among those who are receptive – not "the wise and the intelligent" but those who are childlike ("infants") in their openness to God.

In Sirach, personified Wisdom several times invites those who would be wise to "come to me" and to "put your neck under her yoke", where after toiling a little one may find "much serenity" (Sirach 24.19; 51.23-27). Jesus then identifies himself with that Wisdom (also called the *Logos* or "Word of God") that existed with God from the beginning.

ARCHBISHOP TERRENCE PRENDERGAST

In addressing those who "are weary and are carrying heavy burdens", Jesus has in mind those who are not yet his disciples. His offer of rest, however, is given to all who shoulder his yoke. In Judaism, the "yoke" was a common metaphor for obedience, subordination or servitude. It generally referred to the observance of the Torah – all that God had made known of his purpose – and the keeping of God's commandments.

Here Jesus claims that his teaching is the full revelation of God's will for humanity. In contrast with the teaching of Moses, which Jesus has already deepened (cf. Matthew 5.21-48), Jesus embodies God's purpose and demands. Like Moses, who had been described as the gentlest person on earth (Numbers 12.3), Jesus is "gentle and humble in heart". And, in his servant-like humility, Jesus offers the rest that God long ago had promised through Jeremiah (6.16).

"Rest" does not mean idleness or the absence of activity, but rather a deep sense of peace and well-being amid all the activities that mark the Christian disciple's engagement in family, society and Church. The future dimension of this rest – that Jesus makes available even now in this world – is the fullness of salvation in the world to come. In effect, then, Jesus' invitation and promise here are a summary of the gospel message, as well as the source of much consolation for believers.

Paul offers his own description of the reality spoken of by Jesus. He tells of the Spirit of Jesus now at work in disciples' lives ("you are in the Spirit, since the Spirit of God dwells in you").

The Holy Spirit dwelling in believers' hearts pledges a future risen life with Christ in heaven ("the Spirit of God who raised Jesus from the dead ... will give life to your mortal bodies also through his Spirit that dwells in you").

Fifteenth Sunday in Ordinary Time

The World As God's Parable

* 1st reading: Isaiah 55.10-11
* Psalm: 65
* 2nd reading: Romans 8.18-23
* Gospel: Matthew 13.1-23

Some years back, an Italian film was nominated for an Academy Award. *Il Postino* (The Postman) tells the fictional story of a friendship between the Chilean poet Pablo Neruda and the endearing character who daily brought his mail during the poet's exile in Italy.

In their daily conversations, poet and postman share a great deal. One day, when the postman asks the poet's help in expressing love for a young lady, they speak of metaphors: how the world around us is like human experiences, and how images from nature reflect human life and emotions. When it rains, we may say the sky is weeping. The ebb and flow of ocean waves can stand for the currents of joy and sorrow present in our lives.

The Bible is full of such metaphors and figures of speech. The sacred writers used every form of poetic speech to help illuminate the manner in which human lives connect with the life of God. To a group of Israelites who were back in the Promised Land after their exile and discouraged at the hard labour required to rebuild their society, Isaiah spoke a word of comfort from God.

In effect, God was urging those whose faith was growing slack to remain hopeful. It was as if God urged the Israelites to look at nature. Snow and rain come down from heaven and bring forth abundance from the ground. They make the earth "bring forth and sprout, giving seed to the sower and bread to the one who eats".

Such, God says, is the case with the word I speak to you. If you let it take root in you, it will bring forth a rich harvest ("My word

ARCHBISHOP TERRENCE PRENDERGAST

shall not return to me empty, but it shall accomplish that which I purpose, and succeed in the thing for which I sent it").

When Jesus began proclaiming the kingdom of God, there were many scoffers. What good, they wondered, could possibly come from obscure beginnings in a backwater such as Galilee? Some such situation may have prompted Jesus to challenge the crowds to look over their shoulders at a farmer going out to sow seed in the neighbouring field ("Listen! A sower went out to sow").

As the farmer sows, some seeds are lost and do not produce grain because they have fallen on rocky ground, on shallow soil or among the thorns. And there's a lesson to be gleaned from them about how we prepare ourselves to hear God's word (for example, "what was sown on rocky ground, this is the one who hears the word and immediately receives it with joy; yet such a person has no root, but endures only for a while, and when trouble or persecution arises on account of the word, that person immediately falls away"). Other types of hearing without bearing fruit are also briefly described.

But more noteworthy, Jesus argued, was the seed that fell in good soil. Such seed produces a hundredfold, or sixty or thirty – all extraordinary yields! Just so does God's word take root in our lives. It yields an abundant harvest ("what was sown on good soil, this is the one who hears the word and understands it [because he or she is open to the instruction Jesus gives], who indeed bears fruit and yields ... a hundredfold ... sixty ... thirty").

Aware of the presence of suffering in human lives, Paul said that Christians should imagine the human and created worlds as being involved in one giant act of giving birth ("We know that the whole creation has been groaning in labour pains"). Then, he added, "we ourselves ... groan inwardly while we wait for ... the redemption of our bodies". Paul believed this redemption would take place in the kingdom of God on a day when all people would see themselves as adopted children of God.

To see God at work in nature and in their lives, people need faith – a faith that helps one see beyond the bread and wine offered at Mass. These become, through the Holy Spirit's power, the Body and Blood of the Risen Lord Jesus Christ, which God lovingly gives to his children in the banquet of eternal life. Gladly accepting God's gift of the Eucharist, Christians pray for faith also to see God at work in the world.

Sixteenth Sunday in Ordinary Time

God's Patience Until Harvest Time

* 1st reading: Wisdom 12.13, 16-19
* Psalm: 86
* 2nd reading: Romans 8.26-27
* Gospel: Matthew 13.24-43

If we compare Mark's fourth chapter with Matthew's thirteenth chapter – both of which depict Jesus' parables of the kingdom – we are struck by how much more complex and extensive Matthew's traditions are.

In Matthew's collection, the mustard seed parable gets matched with one about yeast that a woman used to leaven three measures of flour. Matthew remarks that Jesus told the crowd nothing without a parable so as to fulfill prophecy and in order to reveal mysteries "hidden from the foundation of the world".

Finally, unique to Matthew's gospel are the parable of the wheat and the weeds, along with its explanation – as well as the brief parables of the treasure found in a field, the pearl of great value and the dragnet cast into the sea – which will be narrated next Sunday.

Last week, Jesus explained the purpose for his parables: "the reason I speak to them in parables is that 'seeing they do not perceive, and hearing they do not listen, nor do they understand' ... so that they might not look with their eyes, and listen with their ears, and understand with their heart and turn – and I would heal them" (Matthew 13.14-15).

This statement by Jesus, quoting Isaiah 6.9-10, remains puzzling. It seems to suggest that parables have a double purpose. On the one hand, for those who have responded positively to Jesus, the parables communicate further insight and knowledge. But for those who have rejected Jesus and his message, the parables have the effect of causing them to sink further into the dark. In other words, commitment leads to knowledge, but unbelief leads to further ignorance.

But what message do the parables communicate to those who believe in Jesus? Here we note that, like poetry and other works of art, parables contain greater depths of meaning than any single explanation suggests. Still, the parable of the mustard seed seems to suggest that the kingdom of God initially may be as humble as the mustard seed is small, but it is destined for impressive growth like the plant the mustard seed becomes.

Likewise, though Jesus' instruction about God's kingdom is hidden, the transforming power of his gospel is as pervasive as yeast that a woman "took and hid" (the English translation "took and mixed" misses a nuance found in the Greek), thereby completely leavening the three measures of flour and providing enough bread for a great banquet.

The parable of the wheat and the weeds (sown respectively by good and wicked people) suggests that people of lawlessness (the weeds) coexist in this world with the righteous (the wheat). This is so even though Jesus has already announced the inauguration of God's eschatological rule ("the kingdom of heaven").

A dramatic separation will one day take place, but that will not happen "until the harvest" ("the end of the age" or world). While this situation remains perplexing for members of Christ's Church, it calls for both patience and trust in God.

That means patience with the presence of good and bad dwelling together even in the Church – which exists in the world – without rushing to judgments about anyone. After all, as the parable points out, wheat and weeds are hard to distinguish. And it means trust that Jesus, the Son of Man, "will send his Angels, and they will collect out of his kingdom all causes of sin and all evildoers".

The coming Day of Judgment will rectify all matters, and then the righteous will be blessed with extraordinary happiness ("the righteous will shine like the sun in the kingdom of their Father").

The reading from Sirach points out that God's forbearance, or patience with human frailty, is a sign of God's strength ("for you have power to act whenever you choose"). Unlike the manner in which people might want to tackle sin and injustice, God chooses to "judge with mildness", thus caring "for all people".

God's compassion towards the weak is manifest also in the way in which the Holy Spirit helps Christians in their weakness: "the Spirit intercedes with sighs too deep for words".

By letting the Holy Spirit, who dwells in Christians, pray in them, disciples open themselves to God's mindset, "because the Spirit intercedes for the saints according to the will of God".

Seventeenth Sunday in Ordinary Time

Stumbling Across or Seeking the Treasure of God's Kingdom

* 1st reading: 1 Kings 3.5-12
* Psalm: 119
* 2nd reading: Romans 8.28-30
* Gospel: Matthew 13.44-52

Matthew's parable chapter (13.1-52) closes with several units unique to his account of Jesus' teaching. The parable of the "treasure hidden in a field" and of "the pearl of great value" underline the joy of discovering God's kingdom, whether one stumbles across it or goes in search of it.

The dragnet parable continues the theme of judgment "at the end of the age" found in the earlier parable of the wheat and the weeds. Here, however, Jesus does not contemplate the fate of the righteous,

ARCHBISHOP TERRENCE PRENDERGAST

but of those who reject his messianic teaching. "The Angels will come out and separate the evil from the righteous and throw them into the furnace of fire".

Finally, Jesus spoke of a scribe instructed in kingdom values and able to bring "out of his treasure what is new and what is old". Jesus implied that disciples who understood his message qualify as skilled scribes ("Have you understood all this?" They answered, "Yes"). We should understand the "new" as the gospel message. The gospel, however, does not do away with, but fulfills and deepens, the "old" – the Law, prophecy and writings of the Old Testament.

The treasure and the pearl parables appear together in Matthew, but are found nowhere else in the canonical gospels. They appear – though separated from each other – also in the uncanonical *Gospel of Thomas*, an ancient document whose precise age is disputed and which came to light in fragmentary Greek form at the turn of the twentieth century, but in a full Coptic version only in 1945. It is unclear, then, whether the two parables were originally meant to be interpreted in light of each other, as their present location in Matthew's collection of Jesus' teaching suggests.

In favour of interpreting the parables as complementary is their common structure: a brief scene from daily life describes a protagonist who faces a crucial test and decides to sell everything for the sake of one valuable object. Readers should probably understand that it is neither the "treasure" nor the "merchant" that is like the "kingdom of heaven", but the story as a whole with its invitation to its hearers to take action.

The actor in the first parable was going about a daily routine, not looking for anything special and, by accident, came across a treasure hidden in a field. This filled him with joy. By contrast, the merchant knew precisely what he wanted and actively sought it out. The "pearl of great value" that he found, however, exceeded his every expectation. No mention is made of joy at his discovery, but one may imagine it as implied by his decisive response – "he went and sold all that he had and bought it".

Scholars point out that what the merchant did was in keeping with legitimate commercial activity, whereas there are doubts about the legal or ethical propriety of the one who bought land on which buried treasure was found. Roman legal discourse featured discussions about whether one who found hidden treasure on another's property was obliged to report it to the owner. Was someone who bought such a field without reporting it cheating the owner of what was rightly his treasure?

Jesus, however, does not address such concerns. His focus is on the kingdom of heaven as a reality of tremendous worth that others can pass by without noticing. The kingdom can be present in embryonic form in Jesus' ministry, but not be perceived. Those who discover it know that it is worthwhile giving up everything for the joy of having it.

The importance of truly discerning what makes for happiness in this world appears not only in Jesus' parabolic instruction but undergirds Solomon's prayer for wisdom instead of riches. God lavishly answered Solomon's prayer ("I give you a wise and discerning mind"). Later God gave Solomon riches, too.

God-given wisdom helps disciples understand Paul's conviction that "all things work together for good for those who love God, who are called according to his purpose".

God's plan for believers is that they "be conformed to the image of his Son", not only by their death to sin in the waters of baptism, but also by how they live joyfully in this world the life of the kingdom.

Eighteenth Sunday in Ordinary Time

"Eat What Is Good, Delight Yourselves in Rich Food"

* 1st reading: Isaiah 55.1-3
* Psalm: 145
* 2nd reading: Romans 8.35, 37-39
* Gospel: Matthew 14.13-21

n the Bible, the banquet is frequently used as an image to describe God's care for humanity. This explains why, at key moments in history, divine–human relationships get sealed by means of a celebratory or sacrificial meal.

This was the case when Israel came forth from Egypt and at the covenant-making ceremony of Sinai. Biblical sages spoke of coming to dine at the feast as a symbol for imbibing God's wisdom ("Incline your ear, and come to me; listen, so that you may live").

In his ministry, Jesus celebrated friendship meals with outcasts and sinners as a sign that the kingdom of God was breaking into the world in a new way. Likewise, all four gospels depict Jesus feeding crowds in the wilderness with loaves and fish multiplied for thousands. Mark and Matthew depict this wilderness feeding event as occurring twice. Once it appears in a setting with Jewish overtones and, in the second instance, with hints of a Gentile context.

The gestures of Jesus in these feeding miracles (looking up to heaven, blessing, breaking, giving) suggest that the Church saw these privileged moments as anticipations of the sacrificial meal of the Eucharist that Jesus would later leave as a memorial of the "new covenant" in his blood.

Lastly, both Old and New Testaments herald a coming eschatological banquet when, at the end of time and freed from anything that would diminish their joy, God's people would share a meal in total harmony and peace.

Isaiah's oracles of salvation, found in today's first reading, address the situation of the Israelites who were returning to Sion (Jerusalem) after the humiliation of their exile in Babylon. Isaiah proclaimed that the only true "return" – one that included the opening of a door to Israel's Gentile neighbours – was a return to God's ways instead of human ways.

God's way is that of salvation, which is being offered as a free gift: "Come, buy wine and milk without money and without price." It is an offer of the food that God alone gives ("eat what is good, and delight yourselves in rich food"). This fare is the teaching of the word of God that in the ministry of Jesus would foretell his gift of the food that is the Eucharist.

God's nourishing word calls for attentiveness and receptivity. God's victuals, which are true instruction, demand discipline: "Why do you spend your money for that which is not bread, and your labour for that which does not satisfy? Listen carefully to me …". Ultimately, feeding on and clinging to God's instruction is what truly satisfies human hearts ("listen, so that you may live").

Immediately before narrating the multiplication of the loaves for the thousands, Matthew told of King Herod's banquet, which culminated in the beheading of John the Baptist (14.1-12). It is an image of the worst sort of evil that humankind can muster. Faced with the hostile power of the kingdom of this world, Jesus "withdrew in a boat to a deserted place by himself". Jesus did not respond to evil with violence but with a search for solitude, just as, later on, he would seek seclusion for an opportunity to pray (14.23).

The mini-drama of the miracle of the loaves has three parts. It opens with a notice that Jesus had compassion for the crowd "and cured their sick". This so enthralled the people that they were reluctant to leave. Though they are as yet uncommitted to him, Jesus encouraged them to stay with him till evening.

Then comes Jesus' dialogue with his disciples. He challenged them, saying, "you give them something to eat". They do not appear sarcastic, as in Mark's account (6.37), but simply volunteer their lack of resources: "We have nothing here but five loaves and two fish".

Finally, in the miracle, the extravagance of messianic times replaces the hunger of God's people ("all ate and were filled; and they took up what was left over of the broken pieces, twelve baskets full").

As they feed on God's provisions, Christians come to understand Paul's teaching that nothing ("famine, or nakedness, or peril, or sword … nor things present, nor things to come") can separate them "from the love of God in Christ Jesus our Lord".

"We Were with Him on the Holy Mountain"

* 1st reading: Daniel 7.9-10, 13-14
* Psalm: 97
* 2nd reading: 2 Peter 1.16-19
* Gospel: Matthew 17.1-9 or Mark 9.2-10 or Luke 9.28b-36

The second letter of Peter takes the form of a circular letter written to the churches of Asia Minor, which Peter had addressed in his first Letter.

Since the author was skilled in the art of Greco-Roman rhetoric, some scholars are of the opinion that this letter derives from a "Petrine circle" in Rome made up of close associates or disciples of Peter. If this is so, the letter would represent the reflections of a disciple who knew Simon Peter's mind well enough to write in his name.

If Peter wrote the letter using a secretary to formulate his thoughts, it must be dated in the 60s. If, however, it is by a disciple using Peter's name as a pseudonym, the letter could have been written as late as the mid-second century.

The transfiguration of Jesus figures prominently in this writing as a significant spiritual experience. This mysterious mountaintop occurrence grounds the Christian understanding that something still to come – namely, the Parousia of Jesus, described as "the power and coming of our Lord Jesus Christ" – and its accompanying judgment are not "cleverly devised myths".

Rather, Jesus' future coming in glory and judging function constitute truths founded on a spiritual reality that "eyewitnesses" (the apostles Peter, James and John) saw and heard.

---

2   Note: Whenever the Transfiguration displaces a Sunday in Ordinary Time, the Scriptures are invariable, except for the gospel, which is chosen according to the cycle (Year A, B or C).

Belief in the Parousia (sometimes called the "second coming") of Jesus appears regularly in New Testament writings. With the final judgment, it came to be incorporated in credal statements such as the Apostles' Creed ("he will come again to judge the living and the dead"). Often, the Parousia is presented as something about to take place very soon.

When the Parousia did not materialize immediately, some began to doubt it entirely. False teachers in Peter's day questioned the doctrine of the Parousia and whether there would be a divine judgment because of Christ's apparent delay.

The sacred author's answer to the delayed Parousia (something more evident to Christians in the third millennium) was to note that apostolic traditions themselves had said people would tire of the moral life demanded by the gospel and mock true belief: "First of all you must understand this, that in the last days scoffers will come, scoffing and indulging their own lusts and saying, 'Where is the promise of his coming? For ever since our ancestors died, all things continue as they were from the beginning of creation!'" (2 Peter 3.3-4).

The false teachers deny the Parousia because, according to the proclamation of the apostles, the first generation of Christians ("our ancestors") were to have experienced the Parousia but died without its having materialized. In spite of its lateness, the author defends the doctrine that God will intervene in history with judgment of all human actions.

Peter held up the transfiguration as an anticipatory vision of God's installation of Jesus as the end-time divine viceroy. The "Majestic Glory" – a circumlocution for God – quotes Psalm 2.7, a text originally spoken at the installation of a king in Israel, to claim that God was not simply revealing Jesus' kingship but appointing him as Lord and Judge of history. Thus, the transfiguration is the historical basis for God's declaration that Jesus will come as king at the Parousia and exercise sovereignty over all.

The author then goes on to say that apostolic teaching is trustworthy because it relies on Old Testament prophecy. Then he says that believers should know that such scriptural prophecies have

ARCHBISHOP TERRENCE PRENDERGAST

been made more secure because of the transfiguration ("we have the prophetic message more fully confirmed").

Indeed, by being attentive to the coming Parousia, members of the various local churches will be prepared when the true light of Christ comes: "You will do well to be attentive to this as to a lamp shining in a dark place, until the day [of Christ] dawns and the morning star rises in your hearts".

Each evangelist offers an interpretation of the transfiguration. They are summed up in today's Preface: "Christ revealed his glory to the disciples to strengthen them for the scandal of the Cross. His glory shone from a body like our own, to show that the Church, which is the Body of Christ, would one day share his glory".

Nineteenth Sunday in Ordinary Time

Walking on Water

* 1st reading: 1 Kings 19.9, 11-13
* Psalm: 85
* 2nd reading: Romans 9.1-5
* Gospel: Matthew 14.22-33

Perhaps the most dramatic gospel scene featuring Peter is Matthew's portrait of a hero who steps into the waves, then falters through lack of faith. Peter boldly enters upon the water only to sink moments later, at which point Jesus rescues him.

As in Peter's case, greatness and frailty can go hand in hand in a Christian's life. Today, disciples with "little faith" can reach out to Jesus' outstretched hand. Jesus brings them back into the boat with those who bow down to worship him (namely, the members of his Church) and confess, "Truly, you are the Son of God".

In Matthew, Jesus exercises powers and displays qualities traditionally associated with God. When Jesus subdues the sea's upheaval and walks on the sea, he performs deeds attributed to God in the Old Testament. God actively shares with the Son his divine characteristics.

Just as Jesus once walked on the water towards his frightened disciples, Matthew intimates, Jesus will never forget or abandon his own. He comes to deliver from disaster and evil. Though he showed forth only a "little faith", Peter offered an opportunity for Jesus' divine power to be revealed. Through this episode, the individual Christian learns that what counts above all is Jesus' presence, and not merely one's own will and courage. When courage seems to fail believers, Jesus draws near.

The Elijah cycle (1 Kings 17.1–2 Kings 1.18) tells of the prophet's efforts to win Israel back to the ways of God. After initial successes, his enemies were gaining the upper hand. Despondent, Elijah fled far from the northern kingdom, begging God to take his life. God sent heavenly food through an angel. Strengthened by this nourishment, Elijah came to the mountain of God called Horeb (a variant name for Mount Sinai), where God had appeared to Moses.

Readers of the Bible would expect God to come with signs like a storm, earthquake or lightning. But these only herald God's presence. God appeared to Elijah in a light breeze or, as the new translation paradoxically puts it, in "a sound of sheer silence". Believers are reminded by this wording that God is spirit. God deals intimately with his messengers, revealing plans for both judgment and salvation.

The difference between God's coming to Moses on Sinai and to Elijah at Horeb may indicate a shift in biblical understanding about the way God chooses to communicate. At the mountain of God called Sinai, God appeared to Moses in a *visual* way. At the same mountain of God – designated Horeb – God appeared to Elijah in an *auditory* way. People of faith learn that, though the word of God is scarcely audible, it may be more effective than lightning, earthquake or fire.

Paul expressed sadness but no hostility towards what we would call his former co-religionists. Out of love for them, he suggested that he would even be willing to be "accursed and cut off from Christ" – the worst fate he can imagine – if only this would lead to the good "of my own people". This statement is akin to Moses' request that

ARCHBISHOP TERRENCE PRENDERGAST

God blot him out of the Book of Life so that the people of Israel might be forgiven (Exodus 32.32).

Then Paul lists eight of the privileges of Israel: their "adoption" as God's children; the presence of God's "glory" in their desert tent of meeting and Temple in Jerusalem; the "covenants" God made with their patriarchs and families; the expression of God's will given to them in writing through Moses, the Torah or "the giving of the law"; their "worship" of God in the Temple; the "promises" made to Abraham, Moses and David; their ancestral heritage of the "patriarchs"; and, lastly (though they have not accepted Jesus as such), the Messiah "according to the flesh".

Later, as he wrestled over Israel's future, Paul argued that God never takes back his gifts or revokes his choice. For this reason the Jews, as the chosen people, are still the "beloved" of God (Romans 11.28-29). Paul ends his treatment of God's saving plan for the chosen people with praise of God's inscrutable will and designs (11.33-36). The human response to God's saving will is a hymn of praise with Paul: "God be blessed forever. Amen".

Twentieth Sunday in Ordinary Time

A Woman's Extraordinary Faith

* 1st reading: Isaiah 56.1, 6-7
* Psalm: 67
* 2nd reading: Romans 11.13-15, 29-32
* Gospel: Matthew 15.21-28

The post-exilic prophet called "Third Isaiah" (the author of chapters 56 to 66 of the "Book of Isaiah") exercised his divine mandate sometime after King Cyrus's decree permitted Jewish exiles to return to their homeland (539 BC). Like Second Isaiah, whose work – spoken to the Israelite exiles in Babylon between 550 and 539 – is found in chapters 40 to 55, Third Isaiah fostered the spiritual legacy of Isaiah of Jerusalem. This prophetic giant's career flourished between 740 and 701; his oracles and teaching are found scattered in Isaiah, chapters 1 to 39.

Adapting his predecessors' thought to a new era, Third Isaiah addressed those newly returned from the Exile in Babylon to face a devastated Jerusalem. In a marvellous vision, Third Isaiah invited the disheartened refugees to imagine God declaring his imminent creation of a society in which Israel welcomed the inclusion of the Gentile nations. A broad moral commitment rather than specific ritual observances – except that of keeping the Sabbath – would allow people who were not born Israelites to become servants of the Lord and sharers in God's covenant.

God's purpose for well-motivated outsiders – participation in worship on Mount Sion and even in the Jerusalem Temple – was made manifest by the prophet's testimony that "The foreigners who join themselves to the Lord ... I will bring to my holy mountain, and make them joyful in my house of prayer".

Jesus made the powerful closing part of this divine pledge ("my house shall be called a house of prayer for all peoples") the rationale for his prophetic action in, or cleansing of, the Temple during the closing days of his earthly ministry (cf. Mark 11.17).

If in Mark's gospel Jesus seems favourably disposed to Gentiles, matters seem otherwise in Matthew's gospel. There, in his encounter with a Canaanite woman, Jesus observed, "I was sent only to the lost sheep of the house of Israel".

Jesus' aloofness and seeming disregard for the Canaanite woman's feelings evokes consternation among his disciples – perhaps more so today when we are sensitive to the politically correct.

How may one understand Jesus' dismissal of a foreign woman's plea for the healing of a daughter who was "tormented by a demon" ("It is not fair to take the children's food and throw it to the dogs")? First of all, there is a serious issue at stake – that of Jesus' mission to Israel – from which he must not back down. Jesus used the contemptuous Jewish outlook towards Gentiles – the kind of language she would expect – to explain how her request fails to fit in with his mission.

The other point we must note is that a written text cannot reflect the mood of a conversation (a jocular tone or twinkle in the eye). The Canaanite woman agreed with Jesus ("Yes, Lord") but her assent turned into an objection. She explained why this circumstance was unfair and asked whether his mission might not allow others to share in the blessings he brings – even if it is as a secondary effect ("yet even the dogs eat the crumbs that fall from their masters' table").

No one else got the kind of accolade from Jesus that she did ("Woman, great is your faith! Let it be done for you as you wish"). Her faith anticipated the time of the Church when Israel would transcend boundaries of culture and nationality. Israel retains its historical privilege as God's chosen people, but in Christ that grace is shared with the Gentiles.

Paul's closing reflection, in chapters 9 to 11 of Romans, on the relationship of the Church to Israel remains complex. The easiest statement is his conviction that "the gifts and the calling of God are irrevocable". Pope John Paul II, in an address at the Synagogue of Mainz in 1982, spoke in this context about God's covenant with Israel that "has never been revoked". God is faithful to the election of Israel, the Jewish people.

Yet, how God might associate the Jewish people to Jesus, the Messiah, in the plan of salvation remains unfathomable. Paul can only hazard the view that, if their rejection of Jesus meant a blessing to the Gentiles ("the reconciliation of the world"), their acceptance of him must imply "life from the dead". For God's mercy in allowing all people to fall into disobedience is only so that one day God "may be merciful to all".

Twenty-first Sunday in Ordinary Time

Simon Peter's Inspired Confession

* 1st reading: Isaiah 22.15, 19-23
* Psalm: 138
* 2nd reading: Romans 11.33-36
* Gospel: Matthew 16.13-20

saiah speaks of corrupt politics at the court of King Hezekiah around the year 703, when Assyria was advancing on Jerusalem. There a royal official, Shebna, had been found guilty of feathering his own nest by planning a luxurious tomb for himself at a time of national crisis. Moreover, Isaiah criticized him for trying to get Hezekiah to align himself with Egypt against God's designs.

From the prime minister, Shebna, authority over the House of David – symbolized by his bearing the key of the House of David on his shoulder – would be transferred to Eliakim. Though the words are pronounced by Isaiah, it is clear that God is the agent in all these gestures ("Thus says the Lord God of hosts: 'On that day I will call my servant Eliakim … I will commit your authority to his hand'"). Other symbols of authority are also mentioned: the robe and the sash, which would be taken from Shebna and given to Eliakim.

Royal stewards were given immense power ("he shall open, and no one shall shut; he shall shut, and no one shall open"). God promised to establish Eliakim securely, like a peg solidly mounted on a wall that holds all the household needs. He would be expected, with God's help, to bear the weight of every demand that the people of Jerusalem would put on him.

In the gospel, Jesus entrusted responsibility for his future Church to someone who, one might argue, it was questionable that he was able to bear the weight that this would place on his shoulders. Later in the dialogue that Jesus shared with him at Caesarea Philippi, Simon Peter would object to God's design that Jesus fulfill his messiahship by dying on the cross and rising from the dead three days later (as we will hear next Sunday).

But at the moment of his confession that Jesus was "the Messiah, the Son of the living God", Jesus praised "Simon son of Jonah" for his openness to God's inspiration. "For flesh and blood [symbolic shorthand for all that was human and hence perishable] has not revealed this to you, but my Father in heaven'".

And Jesus made a promise to Simon, whom he dubbed "Peter" – a name that means "rock" – that "on this rock" he would build his Church. Christians disagree on the meaning of this statement. Some hold that Jesus meant he would build the Church on the rock of the

ARCHBISHOP TERRENCE PRENDERGAST

faith underlying Peter's confession. Roman Catholics understand Jesus' statement to mean that he intended to build the Church on Simon Peter, a human individual prone to weakness but willing to allow God's power to be at work even in his frailty.

In Luke's gospel, Jesus made a similar promise to Peter as he foretold his coming denials: "Simon, Simon, listen! Satan has demanded to sift all of you like wheat, but I have prayed for you that your own faith may not fail; and you, when once you have turned back, strengthen your brothers" (Luke 22.31-34). Peter's task would be to gather all into unity in the Church so that all could know that they have been forgiven and brought back into God's family.

Jesus entrusted to Simon Peter the sign of authority in the Church: "the keys of the kingdom of heaven" so that "whatever you bind on earth will be bound in heaven, and whatever you loose on earth will be loosed in heaven". Somewhat like a chief rabbi, Peter was given authority by Jesus to teach what is permitted or not permitted in Church life. Catholics believe that the authority entrusted to Peter – the Petrine ministry to unify the Church – is exercised by Peter's successors, the bishops of Rome (or popes).

Jesus wanted all to know that the power of Hades – symbolized by the gates to the underworld, the realm of the dead and of the ungodly – would not win the final victory over the Church, despite setbacks the Church might face from persecution and opposition in this world.

In response to this, the Church can only marvel at God's saving designs and cry out with Paul, "O the depth of the riches and wisdom and knowledge of God! How unsearchable are his judgments and how inscrutable his ways! ... To him be the glory forever. Amen".

Twenty-second Sunday in Ordinary Time

"Small Deaths" Lead to Life

* 1st reading: Jeremiah 20.7-9
* Psalm: 63
* 2nd reading: Romans 12.1-2
* Gospel: Matthew 16.21-27

A friend of mine has long been fascinated with the mystery of death. In university courses he studied this facet of human existence as it has been viewed by philosophers, depicted by poets and artists and considered by theologians through the ages. In research he discovered that the Bible is a rich mine for contemplating death and its corollary, life.

Once he observed that people in our culture tend to flee from giving thought to death: their own death or other experiences of death that come to them in their lives. He is convinced that, paradoxically, people's refusal to allow themselves to face death inhibits them from entering fully into life. For fleeing thoughts of death tends to prevent people from making commitments to life.

Now every choice that one makes in this life – between one good and another – represents, in a sense, a "small death" regarding the path not taken or the good not embraced. Our culture, which fears death, however, urges us to "keep our options open" and not to make a choice or to commit ourselves until we have seen all the possibilities.

Not surprisingly, within this perspective, the longer one puts off a decision – to do some good, to embrace a particular vocation, to love someone or devote oneself to some cause – the harder it becomes for one to decide ultimately in favour of something or of someone, even God.

The word of God constantly urges us to choose the good, to choose the path that leads not to death but to life. Today, Jesus prompts his disciples to see that the pathway to eternal life lies in

ARCHBISHOP TERRENCE PRENDERGAST

dying to self, in taking up the cross, in dying the small deaths leading to life.

Last week, Simon Peter declared the disciples' conviction that Jesus was "the Christ, the Son of the living God" (Matthew 16.16). In today's continuation of that episode, Peter resisted Jesus' prophecy of his coming passion. Peter represents the viewpoint of "Satan" (Hebrew for "adversary", "tempter", "accuser"). Instead of the rock on which Jesus promised to build the Church, Peter appears as a "stumbling block to me" in Jesus' fulfillment of the Father's will.

The paradox of the cross as the way to life is expressed in different formulations in the gospels: believers "denying themselves", taking up the cross and following Jesus; saving one's life by letting go of it; the futility of people "gaining the whole world" if they "forfeit their life" in the process.

Despite commitment to the way of Jesus, it is possible for self-interest, self-will and self-love to get in the way of openness to God's will. At such a point, people must renounce their very selves, their own visions of reality and of what is to their ultimate benefit, and – like Jesus – carry the cross of those sufferings that inevitably form part of life. This practice is done in obedience to the divine wisdom that surpasses every human conception.

This means entrusting one's self to God's provident care, which extends even beyond one's earthly lifespan. In other words, disciples need to see that keeping in touch with God's kingdom and the eternal life it brings is the only satisfactory path to follow.

Paul urged the Romans not to be conformed to the thought patterns of this world. Rather, they were to allow the gospel message to "transform" their lives. The result would be a lifestyle in which they offered their own bodies "as a living sacrifice, holy and acceptable to God".

Jeremiah described the effect of his decision to follow God's way: he became a "laughingstock all day long". He described the way of life he had embraced as a divine seduction. He lamented that God had "enticed" him. He admitted, though, that he had let himself be enticed! Life with God is a challenge – at times frightening – but

Jeremiah would not have had it any other way. Christians pray for courage to embrace that path, as Jeremiah and Jesus did.

The "small deaths" involved in a disciple's day-to-day following of Jesus – carrying the cross – are foolishness to purely human thought patterns. With Christ's guidance, however, they become the path to eternal life.

Twenty-third Sunday in Ordinary Time

Correcting One Another in Love

* 1st reading: Ezekiel 33.7-9
* Psalm: 95
* 2nd reading: Romans 13.8-10
* Gospel: Matthew 18.15-20

When the prophet Ezekiel received his call to proclaim God's word to Israel (2.1–3.15), he received a supplementary call to be a "watchman" (3.16-19). That call is repeated in today's first reading (33.7-9) as well as being elaborated on (33.2-6).

One may imagine a land besieged by an enemy and a sentinel hired to warn of the enemy's approach. If the watchman warns of the army's attack by blowing the trumpet, those who fail to heed the warning are responsible for their lives. But if the watchman fails to blow the trumpet, it is he who has cost the citizens their lives.

It is the same in the spiritual realm. Ezekiel receives God's word warning of death as punishment for sin. The sinful one who neglects this warning is responsible for his or her life and Ezekiel is free of guilt ("if you warn the wicked person to turn from their ways, and they do not turn from their ways, they shall die in their iniquity, but you will have saved your life"). But if Ezekiel gives no warning – when God has called him to do so – he must bear guilt for the sinner's death.

Ezekiel went on to point out the individual person's responsibility for living a godly life. A proverb in Israel stated that "the parents have eaten sour grapes, and the children's teeth are set on edge" (18.2), or one generation sinned but the next generation paid the consequences. Ezekiel refutes this theory. God, he says, does not want any sinner to die. Each person bears personal responsibility for freely turning from sin to an orientation in conformity with God's will (33.10-20).

Jesus' fourth sermon in Matthew's gospel (18.1-35) touches on life in the Church. In Jesus' community, all are called to become, by conversion, like little children (18.1-5). Summoned to personal conversion, Church members share in Ezekiel's office of "watchman". Those in the Church are urged by Jesus not to put stumbling blocks (scandals) in the way of their fellow believers ("the little ones"), but instead to search out straying sheep (18.6-14).

The next several verses constituting today's gospel are a virtual handbook of life in the early first-century Church. The case is envisaged of a Christian who has grievously sinned against another. How is the offender to be reconciled and healed?

Jesus offers a three-fold approach: a first, personal approach to the offending individual "when the two of you are alone", for there is no need to broadcast the offence. If the person listens, repentance and reconciliation ensue ("you have regained" your brother or sister).

But confronting someone with an offence is often ticklish, and a negative reaction can take place ("if the person does not listen"). Then, a new tack must be used ("take one or two others along with you"). They may not have witnessed the offence, but they are witnesses to the efforts at reconciling the estranged community member.

Should the offender not listen to this small party, the one offended is to tell it to the Church. If the offender will not listen even to the Church, an extreme penalty is envisaged: ostracism or excommunication. This penalty was very harsh in earlier days, but its purpose was medicinal – getting the sinner's attention in order to draw him or her back to God's mercy celebrated in the Church.

Jesus elaborated these disciplinary procedures as part of the Church's ministry of "binding and loosing" entrusted to Peter earlier (16.19). And Jesus went on to say that wherever two or three would come together in his name to make such important decisions for the good of souls, he would be there in their midst ("where two or three are gathered in my name, I am there among them").

Paul's concluding exhortation to the Romans was that each Christian "owe no one anything, except to love one another, for the one who loves another has fulfilled the law". Such an assertion is easy to say, but harder to live.

Acting as a watchman for the good of others – in the spirit of Ezekiel – or confronting a wayward sister or brother – in the manner Jesus proposed – shows how difficult it is to live out the "debt" of love in the concrete details of one's life as a fellow disciple in the Church.

Twenty-fourth Sunday in Ordinary Time

Is Forgiving One Another Possible?

* 1st reading: Sirach 27.30–28.7
* Psalm: 103
* 2nd reading: Romans 14.7-9
* Gospel: Matthew 18.21-35

When one hears daily of the re-emergence of tribal conflicts, sectarian divisions and international hostilities, the call of Jesus to forgive may appear naive or impossible.

Peter himself seems to suggest as much when – on our behalf? – he asks his question, "Lord, how often should I forgive my brother or sister if they sin against me? As many as seven times?" This question may echo a rabbinic discussion that argued that a brother or sister could be forgiven a repeated sin three times, but for a fourth offence there was no forgiveness.

ARCHBISHOP TERRENCE PRENDERGAST

Peter may have thought himself exceedingly generous in volunteering a seven-fold forgiveness. But Jesus suggests that anyone who keeps count does not really understand forgiveness. Our translation of Jesus' answer of "seventy-seven times" may actually be on the low side; the Greek text can actually be understood to mean seventy times seven or 490 times!

In Genesis, Lamech boasted that he would outdo Cain's seven-fold vengeance by taking seventy-seven-fold vengeance (Genesis 4.24). Jesus' doctrine says that every instinct to seek vengeance must give way to mercy, which cannot be limited by frequency or quantity. The parable Jesus told to illustrate this teaching explains it by making an outrageous contrast.

Jesus introduces the listener to a person who owed a debt beyond all imagining: ten thousand *talents*. If we consider that the annual income for all of King Herod the Great's territories is said to have been 900 *talents* per year, the amount the first person owed was fantastic. Without any means to pay, he sought mercy. Beyond all expectation, the king replied with compassion.

The forgiven slave met a fellow slave who owed him a considerable sum (100 *denarii* was the equivalent of 100 days' wages), though it was paltry by contrast with what the first man had just been forgiven. The difference in the second case is that a repayment of the debt was certainly possible, and the servant's request for time ("Have patience with me, and I will pay you") reasonable.

When the first slave did not respond to his fellow slave with the compassion he himself had received from the master, the other servants were enraged. This outrage is shared by those who read or hear the parable. One is sympathetic when the other servants' report their displeasure to the king, agreeing with his rebuking final question: "Should you not have had mercy on your fellow slave, as I had mercy on you?"

It is remarkable that this parable is the closing unit in the fourth great block of Jesus' teaching that concerns life in the Church (Matthew 18.1-35). The parable suggests that forgiveness needs always to be practised inside the community of faith, a message that speaks to the polarities found in today's Church.

Christians need to keep forgiving one another! And they are able to do so because they all have first been forgiven by God. Their challenge is to hand that forgiveness on to others, beginning with the community of believers. Paul puts it well: "we do not live to ourselves [alone], and we do not die to ourselves [alone]." Every Christian is related to Christ ("If we live, we live to the Lord, and if we die, we die to the Lord") and, through that common relationship with Christ, to other disciples.

Sirach anticipated the teaching of mutual forgiveness found in the parable and in the petition of the Lord's Prayer, "forgive us our debts, as we also have forgiven our debtors" (Matthew 6.12). He rhetorically poses the same dilemma Jesus did in his teaching: "If one has no mercy toward another like oneself, can one then seek pardon for one's own sins?"

Perhaps therein lies the key to being able to forgive: being able to see – as the servant in the parable did not – that the one who needs mercy is "another like oneself" – someone like me. If one were able to see oneself in his or her neighbour and recognize one's common need for mercy, then, indeed, forgiveness might be possible in our world.

Twenty-fifth Sunday in Ordinary Time

"My Thoughts Are Not Your Thoughts"

* 1st reading: Isaiah 55.6-9
* Psalm: 145
* 2nd reading: Philippians 1.20-24, 27
* Gospel: Matthew 20.1-16

The closing chapter of the Book of Consolation (Isaiah chapters 40–55) sees the prophet trying to answer people's objection that God's plans are incomprehensible. In answer, the Lord's spokesman tried to get his listeners to reorient their mindset, searching earnestly for wisdom from the Lord, who remains close by ("call

ARCHBISHOP TERRENCE PRENDERGAST

upon him while he is near") and rich in mercy ("he will abundantly pardon").

It seemed to Isaiah that human thought patterns tended to be narrow, unable or unwilling to grasp God's outlook. Most disconcerting – to human ways of looking at things – was God's unyielding inclination to forgive. Yet the prophet claimed that God's word expressing this predilection had long been known (48.16-22) and could not fail to be effective (55.10-11). Isaiah challenged his hearers to trust God beyond what their human reasoning could envisage.

This Sunday's Scriptures point out that God's manner of proceeding surpasses human imaginings. God's love, particularly, escapes human logic. And even God's folly proves wiser than human wisdom (cf. 1 Corinthians 1.25).

In keeping with Isaiah's vision, Jesus questioned – especially in his parables – a purely juridical idea of reward. Some Pharisees in his day, for example, stressed the idea of human merit. They believed they had acquired rights over God, that rewards for goodness were due them by God. This theme appears in the reaction of the jealous older brother in the parable, which focuses on his prodigal younger brother (Luke 15.11-32).

The parable of the workers in the vineyard, recounted only by Matthew, depicts the world of the harvest in first-century Palestine. This season stirred hopes in the hearts of workers that they would find employment and wages to support their families. Clearly, the owner of the vineyard anticipated a bumper crop, for he went out to the marketplace several times during the day, and each time hired workers.

To the first ones, hired early in the morning, he offered "the usual daily wage", while to those engaged at nine o'clock, noon and three o'clock, he proposed "whatever is right". He did not specify what he would give those he hired at five o'clock; all he said was, "You also go into the vineyard".

The story takes a provocative turn when the vineyard owner ordered his manager to pay all the workers the usual daily wage, beginning with those who had worked only an hour, then those who had worked part of the day, and ending with those who had worked the whole day.

This is not exactly the fulfillment of the saying "the last will be first, and the first will be last" (Matthew 20.16), but there is a certain reversal of expectations going on in the minds of the labourers that is echoed in the expression.

In fact, the landowner's behaviour provoked those who had worked the full day to grumble against him. When they saw his generosity to the late-arriving workers, they expected that they would get more than the usual day's pay. When this did not happen, one articulated their frustration bitterly, saying, "These last worked only one hour, and you have made them equal to us who have borne the burden of the day and the scorching heat".

The landowner – who represents God, since this is a parable of the kingdom of heaven – said that he had done them no harm, for they were receiving the wage they had agreed to (justice was done). But God goes beyond justice – to love and compassion – which he desires to bestow on the last arrivals and those who worked the partial day: "I choose to give to this last the same as I give to you … are you envious because I am generous?"

Yes, God chooses to bless sinners and folks who are seen as good-for-nothings or who care little about God's will. We may conclude that in saving sinners, God takes nothing away from persons whose lives are marked by goodness!

Paul told his converts that he felt competing desires as he languished in prison: whether to embrace death and be with Christ, or to stay on in this world labouring in the vineyard. If he consulted only his own interests, Paul's preference was to be with Christ. But in the end, he inclined to stay alive in order to help the Philippians.

Twenty-sixth Sunday in Ordinary Time

Christ's Self-Emptying Love

* 1st reading: Ezekiel 18.25-28
* Psalm: 25
* 2nd reading: Philippians 2.1-11
* Gospel: Matthew 21.28-32

When he was governor of Bithynia-Pontus in 112–113 AD, Pliny the Younger wrote a report to the Emperor Trajan that Christians were accustomed to singing hymns "to Christ as to a god". In Ephesians 5.19 and Colossians 3.16, Christians are urged to sing psalms and hymns to the Lord.

There are two great hymnic masterpieces in the New Testament that speak of the mystery of Christ. The first is the hymn to God's Word constantly communicating with humanity and culminating in the Incarnation. This mystery states that God's Word became flesh in Jesus, whose obedient life and saving death enables all people to become "children of God" (John 1.1-18).

The second is today's second reading from Paul's Letter to the Philippians, which extols the self-emptying love of Jesus – his obedience to the Father's will even unto death on the cross – as a model for Christian life (Philippians 2.6-11).

In 1899, a German scholar noticed the rhythmic nature of these verses and suggested that Paul was quoting an early Christian hymn whose subject was Jesus Christ. The first strophe deals with his pre-existent state (verses 6-7a); the second refers to his earthly life (verses 7b-8); and the third to his exaltation (verses 9-11).

What some scholars find striking is that the poem's rhythmic flow is broken by the words "even death on a cross". They attribute this emphasis on the crucifixion to Paul's own hand, since his theology stresses the cross – though it appears to be foolishness to Greeks and a stumbling block to Jews (cf. 1 Corinthians 1.23) – as the central feature of God's saving plan.

Whether Paul himself eloquently wrote of Christ or was quoting the early Church's praise of Jesus, he made the point that our Lord's followers should possess the same outlook he did ("let the same mind be in you that was in Christ Jesus").

For Christ did not seek to take advantage of his divine status ("did not regard equality with God as something to be exploited"). Rather, he emptied himself in two ways. First, he did so by taking on the human condition ("taking the form of a slave, being born in human likeness"), and second, by accepting the full limitations of human life in dying shamefully on the cross ("became obedient to the point of death").

God's response to such a death was to glorify Jesus by giving him "the name that is above every name": "the Lord". This is the very title by which God was known in the Old Testament. All creatures human and angelic ("in heaven and on earth and under the earth") now are subject to Jesus. Every knee must henceforth bend in homage to him. And every tongue must confess that Jesus is Lord. This new, exalted status of Jesus gives glory to God.

Paul says Christians have been blessed abundantly – with "encouragement in Christ", "consolation from [God's] love" and "sharing in the Spirit". Since they have received so much, it is imperative that "selfish ambition or conceit" not be found in their midst. Instead, what Christians should cultivate is the opposite of these. "In humility regard others as better than yourselves ... look not to your own interests but to the interests of others".

If this is to be possible, an ongoing change of heart is necessary. Telling a parable of two sons given a command by their father, Jesus lamented the unwillingness of religious people in his day to accept their need of conversion. They could readily answer Jesus' question, "Which of the two did the will of his father?" They knew it was not the one who said, "'I am going, sir', but ... did not go". Rather, it was the one who said "'I will not', but later ... changed his mind and went" into the vineyard to work, who was truly obedient.

Jesus said people one would not expect – tax collectors and prostitutes – had undergone a religious change of mind, believing the message of John. Surprisingly, however, the religious authorities did not change their minds and come to believe. Instead, they challenged Jesus as they had resisted John the Baptist.

Like the prophet Ezekiel, John and Jesus preached obedience to God's call and belief that God wants all to repent and come to know that those who do so "shall surely live; they shall not die".

Twenty-seventh Sunday in Ordinary Time

The Church as God's Vineyard

* 1st reading: Isaiah 5.1-7
* Psalm: 80
* 2nd reading: Philippians 4.6-9
* Gospel: Matthew 21.33-43

Jesus' Jerusalem ministry consisted in controversies, parables and other teachings showing how his views differed from those of the religious authorities. Whereas in Mark Jesus recounted one parable – that of the vineyard – Matthew depicted Jesus telling three parables (two sons sent to work in the vineyard; vineyard tenants trying to seize it; invitations to a royal wedding banquet).

In linking these parables, Matthew hoped members of the Church would identify with the protagonists. Christians were to recognize themselves in the obedient son (last week's gospel), in the banquet guests (next Sunday's gospel), and as tenants working God's vineyard "who will give him the produce at the harvest time" (today's gospel).

The readings from Isaiah and Psalm 80 illustrate how Israel came to be identified with the vineyard motif. Isaiah's "Song of the Vineyard" had an enormous influence on biblical thought. Perhaps sung at the autumn vintage time of mirth and celebration, the song tells what happened to a vineyard that belonged to the prophet's friend ("my beloved").

The prophet sang on the friend's behalf. He told how the vineyard owner did everything necessary to succeed in viniculture ("he dug it and cleared it of stones, and planted it with choice vines"). He made it secure ("he built a watchtower in the midst of it"). Having "hewed out a wine vat in it", he had high hopes the grapes would be lush and the wine sweet.

Instead, the vineyard produced "wild grapes" and sour wine. The disappointed owner ("what more was there to do for my vineyard that I have not done in it?") decided to let the vineyard go to rack and ruin. Once the soliloquy begins ("and now"), one discovers it is no longer the prophet speaking, but God who has sent him ("I will also command the clouds that they rain no rain upon it"). If God – the prophet's "beloved" – is the vineyard owner, then Israel must be the vineyard that has produced "bloodshed" and "a cry" instead of the fruits God expected ("justice" and "righteousness").

Psalm 80 illustrates how the story of the planted vine mirrored God's choice of Israel. "You brought a vine out of Egypt" evokes the Exodus; "you drove out the nations", the conquest of the land of Canaan; and "it sent out its branches to the sea, and its shoots to the River", the growth of David's kingdom from the Mediterranean to the Euphrates. The image of the vine suggests that none of this came about by chance, but by God's commitment to Israel, as a vinedresser is committed to and nurtures the vineyard.

As God had questioned Israel in Isaiah's song, so in the psalm Israel queries God and asks for a change of heart ("Turn again, O God of hosts" really means "repent or have a change of heart, O God" … "have regard for this vine, the stock that your right hand planted").

When Jesus told his parable of the vineyard, one may assume that his hearers would notice echoes of the Old Testament and perceive the meaning of Jesus' commentary on the current situation. Tension arises in Jesus' parable from the fact that the owner was an absentee landlord who wanted all the produce at harvest time. You see, God claims exclusive control over the works of justice the vineyard workers are to produce. God sends messengers – the prophets – to make this demand. Probably the two delegations stand for the pre- and post-exilic prophets (Judaism refers to "former" and "latter" prophets).

The highlight of God's intervention is sending the Son. In Matthew's account, the tenant workers cast the heir outside the vineyard and then kill him, just as in the passion Jesus was taken outside Jerusalem and killed. Remarkably, the parable itself gives no hint of his resurrection. That comes in Jesus' citation of Scripture: "the stone that the builders rejected has become the cornerstone", a parabolic allusion to his resurrection.

The upshot of the parable is that new workers are called to produce "the fruits of the kingdom", the new name for the vineyard of God. Since Jesus' resurrection, the kingdom consists of Jews and Gentiles who form the Church and fulfill God's call to produce a harvest of justice, the fruits or good works that glorify God.

Twenty-eighth Sunday in Ordinary Time

"Come to the Wedding Banquet"

* 1st reading: Isaiah 25.6-10a
* Psalm: 23
* 2nd reading: Philippians 4.12-14, 19-20
* Gospel: Matthew 22.1-14

At the approach of Thanksgiving, the Scriptures speak about feasting on "rich food" and with "well-aged wines". The Psalmist praises the Lord for anointing "my head with oil", while Jesus recounts the parable of a wedding banquet given by a king "for his son". God's word today also challenges those who hear it to be ready to attend the great feast that God will give in the end times.

Ancient literature made frequent use of the image of a great banquet. The last book of the Bible describes the "wedding feast of the Lamb", to which news of Christ's victory over the enemies of God's people is attached (Revelation 19.1-21).

Similarly, the Apocalypse of Isaiah (chapters 24-27) declared that at the end of time, God would remove grief and mourning from people's lives, and indeed would "swallow up death forever". With the fear of death removed and life with God assured ("let us be glad and rejoice in his salvation"), God's children will joyfully partake in the "feast of rich food" prepared "for all peoples".

The social world in which Jesus lived was highly stratified. The elite did not mix or dine with their inferiors. It was not unusual for double invitations for a banquet to be sent out. If the right individuals were coming, all would make a point of attending; if the "right people" stayed away, so would everyone else, and trivial excuses would be proffered.

Those dissatisfied with the wedding banquet arrangements not only showed their disapproval, they shamed the king by murdering his slaves. The king's avenging of his honour would be taken for granted.

But this king's wedding banquet – since it reflected the "kingdom of heaven" – went beyond the conventions of the day. The king decided to invite others to the wedding banquet – people decidedly different from the first ones called ("those invited were not worthy … go to the main streets and invite everyone you find").

Those who see an allegory of salvation history in the parable interpret the first sets of slaves as the prophets. If we regard the final invitation to the wedding banquet as reflecting Jesus' ministry, the last messengers would be the apostles of Jesus. Those summoned are "both good and bad". This reflects the mystery of the Church, where those judged unworthy by traditional religious categories gather. For Jesus accepted "tax collectors and sinners" – those on the margins, the outcast. With Jesus' proclamation, God's messianic banquet becomes fully subscribed!

Now a king who invited the non-elite to his banquet may have supplied wedding garments for any poor unable to provide these for themselves. So, the king, pleased that the banquet hall was full, went in to see the guests his slaves had enlisted. Amidst his joy, he was embarrassed by one individual who, strangely, had not donned a wedding garment. The king, calling this man "Friend", asked how he could have acted in this way. The man remained speechless, and then heard the king call for his expulsion.

In early Christianity, a believer's new identity – through conversion – was symbolized by the putting on of a new set of clothing. Thus, some have seen in the guest's refusal to put on a wedding garment his rejection of the change of life implicit in his accepting the invitation of God proclaimed by Jesus.

The mysterious saying "many are called, but few are chosen" reflects a problem of the Hebrew language created by its lack of comparative adjectives. Comparisons have to be expressed by "large" and "small" or "many" and "few". So, we can understand the passage to mean the chosen are fewer than those called. Jesus did not intend to speak of the actual number of those saved. He simply observed that not all those called will, in the end, be chosen – that is, saved.

Paul praised the Philippians for their care of him in his moments of need. They had helped him both financially and with their encouragement. The ups and downs of his life, Paul said, taught him to live with little and with plenty. "In any and all circumstances I have learned the secret of being well-fed and of going hungry". What was the key to Paul's equanimity? "I can do all things through him [the risen Christ] who strengthens me".

Twenty-ninth Sunday in Ordinary Time

Politics, Religion and Jesus

* 1st reading: Isaiah 45.1, 4-6
* Psalm: 96
* 2nd reading: 1 Thessalonians 1.1-5
* Gospel: Matthew 22.15-21

For several weeks, the gospel reading has featured Jesus telling parables. Now, as Jesus' Jerusalem ministry draws to a close, the Pharisees engage him in controversies.

This week, Jesus is asked whether it is right to pay the poll tax to Caesar. Next week, the defining issue is the greatest commandment in the Law. In both instances, his questioners test Jesus. In each case, his brief reply amazed those who challenged him.

Once the Pharisees concluded that Jesus had them in mind in telling his parables ("they realized Jesus was speaking about them"), they sent their disciples and some Herodians to trap him. Despite protestations of admiration for his integrity ("We know that you are sincere, and teach the way of God in accordance with truth, and show deference to no one …"), they sought to place him on the horns of a dilemma he could not escape.

The hated poll tax, instituted in 6 AD when Judea became a Roman province, fanned the flames of nationalist opposition to the occupying power. Out of such sentiments came the Zealot movement, which fomented the Jewish War of 66–70, which ended in disaster. In principle, the Pharisees resisted the poll tax, while the Herodians – bit players in this drama – openly supported the Romans and favoured paying the tax.

If Jesus supported paying tribute to Caesar, he would be discredited as a prophet. If, however, he argued against paying the tax, this could be used later to portray him to the Romans as a dangerous revolutionary. Jesus saw through their pretence, and asked for the coin used to pay the tax (in this case, a Roman coin was obligatory). He inquired about the image and inscription found on the coin.

Many Jews considered the coin blasphemous. For in having a human representation, it violated the commandment against graven images. Its inscription ("Tiberius Caesar, august son of the Divine Augustus, high priest") made a claim that rivalled God's exclusive sovereignty over Israel. Jews should rightly have wanted to be rid of this coin. Still, they could produce one, whereas Jesus could not.

Jesus, who had expressed willingness to pay the Temple tax to avoid scandal (Matthew 17.4), was not unwilling that the poll tax be paid to Caesar ("Give therefore to Caesar the things that are Caesar's …"). But Jesus went a step further when he added, "and to God the things that are God's".

This claim, we should note, is all-inclusive, for God's image and likeness are found inscribed on all God's subjects. Therefore, all of a believer's life should be rendered to God, while only a paltry coin is owed the civil ruler.

The role of religion or the Church in politics is always a contentious issue. What is clear is that Christian citizens have a right to participate in the secular realm and its political processes.

Religious persons and the Church, then, are duty-bound to remind civic rulers of the dignity of the human person, who bears God's image and likeness. This significant truth will have wide repercussions in spheres such as health care – from the moment of a person's conception to his or her natural death – as well as in areas such as education, corrections, taxation and, indeed, all manner of social policy.

A positive view of political power is presented in the reading from Second Isaiah, in which Cyrus is called God's anointed. Cyrus would enable the Israelites to return to Jerusalem and rebuild the Temple and Holy City. By his divinely sanctioned action on the world stage, he would cause Israel's God to be glorified ("I arm you, though you do not know me, so that all may know ... that there is no one besides me").

Paul summoned the Christian community to let the life of God become manifest in their lives. He praised the Thessalonians for their response to God's saving action in their midst: "We always give thanks to God for all of you ... constantly remembering ... your work of faith and labour of love and steadfastness of hope in our Lord Jesus Christ". For God sent the Holy Spirit among believers to ensure that the message of Jesus would flourish "not in word only, but also in power".

Thirtieth Sunday in Ordinary Time

Jesus' Commandment to Love

* 1st reading: Exodus 22.21-27
* Psalm: 18
* 2nd reading: 1 Thessalonians 1.5c-10
* Gospel: Matthew 22.34-40

When God made a covenant at Mount Sinai with Moses and the Israelite people who had been rescued from Egypt (Exodus 19–24), it was expressed by means of covenantal prescriptions or commandments.

The commandments mentioned in today's first reading stress God's concern for several categories of poor people (the resident alien, the orphan, the widow). God declared that he would as surely hear them ("I will surely heed their cry") as he had answered Israel's pleas in their affliction.

God indicated a special predilection for the poor in time of difficulty. They were not to be treated by their fellow Israelites as one might deal with a creditor. Nor was interest on a loan to be exacted from them. Above all, compassion was to be shown the needy ("if you take your neighbour's cloak in pawn, you shall restore it before the sun goes down; for it may be their only clothing to use as cover").

The stipulated reason for all this was God's declared disposition of mercy ("for I am compassionate"). Clearly, then, compassion had to be a characteristic of God's people, especially in their dealings with the neediest members of society.

As Israel's history developed, so too did reflection on the meaning of the Law God had given. One form of such interest led to the practice of counting commandments and weighing their importance. Thus, God's commandments were said to total 613. They were divided into 248 positive commands (which someone associated with the sum of bodily parts) and 365 negative commands (one for each day of the year).

ARCHBISHOP TERRENCE PRENDERGAST

Some Jews argued that the "moral law" was more important than the "ceremonial law". Others made a distinction between "weighty" and "light" commandments. While none could be neglected because all came from God, some commandments were judged more important than others. For example, the commandment against taking innocent life (Deuteronomy 5.17) seemed to carry more weight than, let us say, the prohibition against boiling a kid in its mother's milk (Deuteronomy 14.21).

It was inevitable, then, that people should have engaged Jesus in the type of discussion we find in today's gospel. In Mark's account, the matter is treated as a friendly discussion by religious scholars, whereas in Luke's gospel the lawyer's question prompts Jesus to tell the story of the Good Samaritan. In Matthew's presentation of this issue, the Pharisee is said to be a "lawyer" (the equivalent of a trained theologian today) with malicious intent: that of entrapping Jesus ("asked him a question to test him").

In replying to the question "Teacher, which commandment in the Law is the greatest?" Jesus cited part of the *Shema'* (Deuteronomy 6.4-5), the credal formula that pious Israelites recited every day at that time (and still do today): "You shall love the Lord your God with all your heart, and with all your soul". The passage continues on "and with all your might", but Jesus' version reads "with all your mind".

One should not exaggerate this difference, for both versions stress total devotion to God with all that a person has and is. In biblical thought, the "heart" was the centre of one's knowing and willing, as well as of one's feeling. The "soul" and "mind" stood for one's entire life and energies. Thus, love entailed not only feeling but, more importantly, doing.

Since God is the centre of all, love of God must be "the greatest and first commandment". But Jesus went beyond his questioner's expectations and added a "second" commandment: "You shall love your neighbour as yourself" (cf. Leviticus 19.18, 34). God must come first, but there can be no true love of the unseen God without love, as well, of the neighbour who can be seen (cf. 1 John 4.20).

What God wills, then, is love. This is the summary not only of the law but, Jesus says, the message of the prophets, too ("On these two commandments hang all the Law and the Prophets"). Thus, God's entire will, as manifested in the Scriptures, may be summed up in Jesus' double commandment of love.

The Alleluia verse shows how the fulfillment of love leads to participation in the very life of God ("The one who loves me will keep my word, and my Father will love him and we will come to him").

Thirty-first Sunday in Ordinary Time

"Have We Not All One Father?"

* 1st reading: Malachi 1.14–2.2, 8-10
* Psalm: 131
* 2nd reading: 1 Thessalonians 2.7-9, 13
* Gospel: Matthew 23.1-12

"Malachi" means "my messenger" and is derived from a passage (3.1) where an end-time precursor is announced ("behold, I am about to send my messenger"). This anonymous prophet toiled between the re-establishment of the Jerusalem Temple in 515 BC and the mission of Nehemiah in 445 BC.

Malachi was zealous to correct abuses in Israel: overly political priests, abuses in liturgy (people offering defective animals in sacrifice), intermarriage with foreigners, and the spread of social injustices. The early Church believed Malachi's vision of God's precursor to have been fulfilled in John the Baptist, who went ahead of Jesus. The Council of Trent understood Malachi's conception of a pure universal offering (1.11) to have been fulfilled in the Eucharist.

Malachi appeals to the common fatherhood of God shared by Israelites as a reason to shun intermarriage with foreigners. For Israelite men were divorcing their wives to marry foreign women who worshipped other gods. Malachi conceived marriage as a covenantal bond instead of a contract that could end in divorce. He anticipated

ARCHBISHOP TERRENCE PRENDERGAST

the exalted vision of the spousal union and the abhorrence of divorce that was to be the hallmark of Jesus' teaching on marriage.

By contrast with the callousness and nonchalance of the priests of Malachi's day, Paul stands out because of his gentleness as he came to visit the Thessalonians ("we were gentle among you, like a nurse tenderly caring for her own children"). Paul saw his vocation to be not only one of sharing the good news with his converts, but, to the extent possible, his very life and self.

The credibility of its messenger, Paul, made the good news attractive in Thessalonica – so much so that, when Paul preached, his converts perceived his message "not as a human word but as what it really is, the word of God, which is also at work in you believers". Paul gave greater credibility to his message by the way he laboured among his converts for their benefit ("we worked night and day, so that we might not burden any of you while we proclaimed to you the Gospel of God").

What Malachi yearned for and Paul practised, Jesus took up in the closing words of his public ministry. Because they had been constituted religious leaders, Jesus said that the scribes and Pharisees were to be followed in what they said. But not in what they did. Jesus went on the offensive against an aspect of their religiosity that he considered bankrupt.

The twenty-third chapter of Matthew's gospel contains one of the most searing addresses in all the New Testament. In the opening part of his public teaching (the Sermon on the Mount), Jesus had given an extended number of beatitudes, declaring blessed those who were poor in spirit, mourning, hungering and thirsting for righteousness, and so on. Now he was castigating religious leaders who "tie up heavy burdens, hard to bear, and lay them on the shoulders of others; but they themselves are unwilling to lift a finger to move them".

How has all of this come to pass? People – and particularly their leaders – have forgotten about humility. Jesus enunciated a paradoxical formula about this spiritual disposition ("whoever exalts himself will be humbled, and whoever humbles himself will be exalted").

Jesus gave several examples of outlooks that militate against the lowliness he espoused. One was the desire to be noticed: "They do all their deeds to be seen by others; ... They love to have the place of honour at banquets and the best seats in the synagogues and to be greeted with respect in the marketplaces".

Another outlook contrary to humility is the love of titles: yearning to be called "rabbi" or "father" or "instructor". What disciples of Jesus should remember is their common enterprise in learning from Jesus, the one teacher or instructor, the Messiah. And they should also recall that all are related to God – "for you have one Father – the one in heaven".

The final antidote to an exalted impression of oneself is the ideal of service: "the greatest among you will be your servant". Eschewing externals (titles and honour and acclaim) and the cultivation of an interior outlook of lowliness, humility and service helps disciples become more like their master, Jesus Christ.

All Saints – November 1

The Challenge of Becoming Saints

* 1st reading: Revelation 7.2-4, 9-14
* Psalm: 24
* 2nd reading: 1 John 3.1-3
* Gospel: Matthew 5.1-12a

Biblical usage of the terms "holy ones" and "saints" applies these terms to all who are distinct because of their relationship with God. One Hebrew term suggests that those associated in covenantal faithfulness are bound to God in love (cf. Psalms 31.23; 148.14). Another Hebrew term ("holy") identified God's people as "set apart" and dedicated to service of the divine (cf. Daniel 7.27).

In the New Testament, the term "saints" regularly translates the term for "holy ones". Generally, it refers to Christians in contrast with unbelievers (cf. 1 Corinthians 6.2). Paul uses the term "saints" interchangeably with those who are "God's beloved", all who are "called to belong to Jesus Christ" (Romans 1.6-7). In the Book of

ARCHBISHOP TERRENCE PRENDERGAST

Revelation, the term "saints" is frequently used to refer to Christian martyrs (17.6).

In other words, the term "the saints" is an appropriate designation for Christians. The Second Vatican Council reflected this doctrine in its declaration that God's call to holiness is universal. Sanctity is the vocation of each disciple of Christ.

Thus, while today's solemnity of All Saints praises God for all who have been recognized by the Church, it may serve as an occasion for Catholics to consider their own personal calls to be God's holy ones in the contemporary world.

The Beatitudes – the charter of rights and obligations of the members of the people of God – reflect both God's initiative and human response in the process of holiness. If they are taken as the admission standard for the kingdom of heaven, it is clear that no one would qualify. But if they are seen as gifts of God, to which each disciple responds in his or her life, they are stimuli to Christians to live up to the challenges God sets before them.

While I generally prefer literal translations of scriptural texts, I must confess that I have always been fond of the New English Bible's dynamic equivalence translation of the first beatitude, "how blest are those who know their need of God [blessed are the poor in spirit], the Kingdom of Heaven is theirs".

Unless one experiences a hunger for eternal life that only God can satisfy, one cannot be open to the gift of the kingdom that God freely gives. This notion is also at the heart of the second beatitude: "blessed are those who mourn, for they will be comforted" [by God].

The experience of grief, through the loss of a loved one, leaves a person feeling terribly vulnerable, hollow, empty – a state that God ultimately transforms with the gift of divine consolation.

As they live in a state of constant receptivity to God's blessings, believers find themselves being transformed from within. As disciples individually live with an openness to God's gift of the kingdom, their human hearts are gradually purified. They begin to wish for others what they themselves have received: "Blessed are those who hunger and thirst for righteousness, for they will be filled. ... Blessed are the pure in heart, for they will see God".

As the Christian lives out the call of the Beatitudes, he or she becomes ever more like Christ, the chief exemplar of the kingdom. This is the point made by the author of the first Letter of John: "we are God's children now; what we will be has not yet been revealed. What we do know is this: when he is revealed, we will be like him, for we will see him as he is".

Through the outlook of the Beatitudes, Christians are enabled to live as Jesus did, even to embracing persecution and suffering as he did ("Blessed are you when people revile you and persecute you and utter all kinds of evil against you falsely on my account. Rejoice and be glad, for your reward is great in heaven").

This perspective on suffering has given joy to persecuted Christians through the centuries. Nowhere is this vision so embraced as in the Book of Revelation, written at the height of Roman oppression against Christians in the late first century ("These are they who have come out of the great ordeal; they have washed their robes and made them white in the blood of the Lamb").

The victory of holiness is God's, but it is realized in those who welcome it with joy.

The Commemoration of All the Faithful Departed (All Souls) – November 2

In Hope of the Resurrection

* 1st reading: Isaiah 25.6-9
* Psalm: 23
* 2nd reading: 1 Corinthians 15.12-26
* Gospel: Mark 8.27-35 or John 1.1-5, 9-14[3]

---

3 Note: The readings for the Commemoration of All the Faithful Departed are drawn from the Scriptures permitted for Christian funerals. Those proposed here have been chosen to address the general issue of prayers for the deceased and the Christian disciple's hope in the resurrection.

ARCHBISHOP TERRENCE PRENDERGAST

All Souls' Day is closely related to the Solemnity of All Saints on November 1. Its observance began at the abbey of Cluny under St. Odilo. In his view, prayer for the dead (that they "rest in peace") with celebration of the saints showed more fully Catholic belief in the communion of saints (those on earth, in purgatory, in heaven).

Christians have remembered their dead from earliest times. Third-century writers spoke of an intermediate place of rest where the faithful awaited God's final judgment. Monica, in dialogue with Augustine at Ostia, where she lay dying, told her son not to worry about her burial place, asking only that he remember her at the Eucharist.

Many Scriptures – especially the early ones – lack clear expectations of life after death. All who die – good or bad – descended to the shadowy netherworld called *Sheol*. Pious Israelites took comfort that their names lived on in their posterity and their remembrance through membership in the people of Israel.

A number of psalms bristled at this common fate of humanity: "Like sheep they are appointed for Sheol; Death shall be their shepherd/ Sheol shall be their home" (Psalm 49.14). The Psalmist called on God for rescue; intimations of an ongoing life with God began to take shape: "But God will ransom my soul from the power of Sheol (Psalm 49.15); "My flesh and my heart may fail, but God is the strength of my heart and my portion forever" (Psalm 73.26).

Gradually, God communicated a future full of hope, beyond death and the grave, for his faithful ones. This truth is boldly asserted in the Isaian Apocalypse (Isaiah 24–27), a work associated with the prophecies of Isaiah of Jerusalem. Its climax is a proclamation of the resurrection: "Your dead shall live, their corpses shall rise. O dwellers in the dust, awake and sing for joy!" (26.19)

God's provident care reassured believers that the resurrection life was not a resumption of the life they lived on earth, even if the life to come has affinities with it. Continuity between earthly and heavenly life is symbolized by the images of banquet food and drink ("the Lord of hosts will make for all peoples a feast of rich food, a feast of well-aged wines").

Still, the future life with God differs notably from life in this world. It will be a new life in a new world, one where the sense of loss and grief will exist no longer: "[God] will destroy on this mountain the shroud that is cast over all peoples, the [winding] sheet [of death] that is spread over all nations; he will swallow up death forever".

Paul faced a situation in Corinth where some Christians denied the future resurrection of the body. Ambivalence among Christians about the risen life in store for them may explain Paul's odd logic as we decipher his argumentation. He said that if God cannot raise the dead ("if there is no resurrection of the dead"), then Christ has not been raised and Paul has been discovered misrepresenting God ("because we testified of God that he raised Christ – whom he did not raise if it is true that there is no resurrection from the dead").

After showing the stunning consequences of false conceptions of the resurrection (15.12-19), Paul laid out the orthodox understanding of the union of Christ and Christians as "children of the resurrection" (cf. Luke 20.36).

Paul made use of the notions of "corporate personalities", Adam and Christ. Adam, through his disobedience to God, sowed the seeds of death, which touches every human being ("all die in Adam"), while Christ, by his obedience to God's design, made it possible for all people to inherit eternal life ("all will be made alive in Christ").

God has an ordered plan. We can imagine a full harvest of faithful believers being brought into God's granary, if we realize that Christ is the first fruits who sanctifies his brothers and sisters, after having been presented as the first of the harvest through his resurrection from the dead ("Christ the first fruits, then at his coming [the Parousia] those who belong to Christ").

Christ's reign will endure until all God's enemies are defeated, the last of which is death ("the last enemy to be destroyed is death").

Thirty-second Sunday in Ordinary Time

Yearning for the Lord's Coming

* 1st reading: Wisdom 6.12-16
* Psalm: 63
* 2nd reading: 1 Thessalonians 4.13-18
* Gospel: Matthew 25.1-13

Wedding customs change imperceptibly over time. But they also delight the generations because they are bearers of ethnic, social and religious traditions.

As weddings draw near in North America, there are showers for the bride and stag parties for the groom. There is ritual in the rehearsal at the church, and the family gathering afterwards. Roles are set down for bridesmaids, the maid of honour and the best man. Even children are involved as ring bearers or altar servers. These customs say something about who we are and what we value.

A few decades ago, the film *Wedding in Galilee* showed how a marriage ceremony could serve as a mirror to the issues of contemporary Palestinian society. In the film's storyline, an Arab patriarch asks the Israeli military governor to lift curfew in the village to celebrate his son's marriage without restraint. The official agrees on condition that he and his retinue be guests of honour.

When the old man reports back on the conditions in which the celebration will take place, there is great turmoil. How can one rejoice when reminders of oppression will be at the head table? Nonetheless, the scenario unfolds and all the underlying societal issues come to the fore: the linking of families, the hope for new life, the paradoxes and conflicts of every day.

The potential for a wedding to bring out underlying values or issues may have been behind Jesus' telling of the parable of ten bridesmaids. To all intents and appearances, the ten are the same. They have come to the wedding. Their lamps are aglow. They are all wearing their bridesmaids' dresses. All fall asleep.

Still, Jesus had observed from the beginning, "five of them were foolish, and five were wise"! Only some future event will reveal the consequences of this division and hint at why some were foolish, others wise.

When the bridegroom's delay ends, the foolish are found to be without oil in their lamps. In the light of what Jesus has taught throughout the gospel, "having oil" on the part of the wise must stand for deeds of love and mercy in obedience to Jesus' great commandments of love (cf. Matthew 22.37-40). As Jesus remarked earlier, "Not everyone who says to me, 'Lord, Lord' will enter the kingdom of heaven, but only the one who does the will of my Father in heaven" (7.21).

The delay of the bridegroom took on pertinence for the early Church. Some, such as those in Thessalonica to whom Paul wrote, thought the Parousia (the "coming in glory") of Christ was near in time. When family members and friends died before Christ's return, they began to read their deaths as a sign of God's judgment and of their exclusion from the kingdom. Not so, Paul replied. "We who are alive, who are left until the coming of the Lord" – we cannot tell here whether Paul actually expected to live until the Parousia or is using "we" to mean the collective Christian community – will have no advantage over those who are "the dead in Christ".

The upshot of all Paul teaches is that, after what happens at the Parousia, "we will be with the Lord forever". This should be a consolation to those who worry about death ("Therefore, encourage one another with these words").

"These words" contain some striking images: "a cry of command", "the archangel's call", "and the sound of God's trumpet". The studies of a Jesuit biblical scholar from Toronto, Fr. Joseph Plevnik, conclude that Paul adapts images taken from the Old Testament's "holy war" tradition to describe God's victory over "death", the last enemy of God's people to be destroyed.

God's triumph over death began in the resurrection of Jesus ("we believe that Jesus died and rose again"). Its corollary is the extension of that victory in the persons of all believers ("through Jesus, God will bring with him those who have died"). Until that victory is complete, Christians need to heed Christ's invitation: "Keep awake, therefore, for you know neither the day nor the hour".

Because yearning for Christ's coming is the bedrock of a believer's faith, he or she must learn to make their own the prayer of Christians from the past: "Maranatha! Come, Lord Jesus!" (Revelation 22.20).

The Dedication of the Lateran Basilica – November 9

"You Are God's Building, God's Temple"

* 1st reading: Ezekiel 47.1-2, 8-9, 12
* Psalm: 46
* 2nd reading: 1 Corinthians 3.9b-11, 16-17
* Gospel: John 2.13-22

I shall never forget my visit several years ago to the Sanctuary of Dan in the upper reaches of the Galilee. Our guide brought us to a damp spot near the altar where a tiny rivulet broke the earth's surface.

Moving away from this source, we noticed that the water increased in volume and sound until, a few hundred metres away, it became a torrent. The energy of the waters' mass stirred exhilaration in us as we gaped at the river that issued from the sacred compound of ancient times. We could not help but make associations with the vision of Ezekiel.

Exiled to Babylon in 573 BC, Ezekiel received a vision of the restored Temple of Jerusalem. The stream of water rising from a hidden spring under God's house may represent the mythical cosmic river that flows from the Temple, the centre of the world. Deeper and sweeter as it moves from the Temple, the river takes away even the brackish taste of the Dead Sea.

The sacred river's course passes through regions that are increasingly barren. As the waters flow, they bring life and healing. The marvellous trees on the river's banks bear fresh fruit crops each month and their foliage remains verdant. The images of Ezekiel's vision constitute a return to Paradise.

The waters of baptism and the gift of the Holy Spirit allow Christians to see Ezekiel's vision being realized in the life of the Church, God's end-time temple.

Paul discussed rivalries in the Church of God at Corinth. Some espoused Cephas (Peter), others Apollos, others Paul; still others claimed to have allegiance only to Christ (1 Corinthians 1.12-13). Correcting them, Paul pointed to God as the one giving growth, after the planting by Paul and the watering of Apollos.

Paul pleaded for unity by urging people to see that they were simultaneously God's field and God's building. If Christians truly are God's building, then that building must be a temple, for "God's Spirit dwells in you".

The temple of God's people can be based only on Christ, who is firm ground ("no one can lay any foundation other than the one that has been laid; that foundation is Jesus Christ"). In speaking about building on the foundation – making ourselves one with Christ – Paul urged each to give their best, their total selves.

No one, then, should be divisive or contribute to tearing down the temple of God, but work only for its upbuilding. Don't destroy yourselves by bickering or disharmony, Paul said, for "God's temple is holy, and you are that temple".

The four gospels recount a prophetic action by Jesus in the temple precincts. It is known as the "cleansing" of the temple. The Fourth Gospel's account of Jesus' temple action gives it a particular colouring through the enigmatic word of Jesus in reply to people asking him on what authority he was acting ("destroy this temple, and in three days I will raise it up").

Ironically, people understood Jesus to be referring literally to Herod's Temple – under construction for 46 years – while he spoke of the "temple" of his body. Jesus was declaring the end of the Temple and its sacrificial system as the way to God. He inaugurated a new way to God through his death on the cross ("destroy this temple") and his resurrection ("in three days I will raise it up").

The key element of such interpretation would derive from his disciples' future act of "remembering" ("after he was raised from the dead, his disciples remembered that he had said this"). This kind of remembering means more than merely recalling Jesus' words or deeds to mind; "remembering" includes perceiving the deeper import of Jesus' words and deeds.

God's holy people, incorporated into the Body of Christ through his death and their association with him in baptism, constitute the new temple in which all have access to God on intimate terms.

This is the central truth celebrated in today's feast. Occasioned by the anniversary of the dedication of the Cathedral Church of Our Saviour and St. John the Baptist (Rome's papal Basilica of St. John Lateran), it is the worldwide celebration of the temple made up of all the baptized, united to Christ – the new temple of the living God.

Thirty-third Sunday in Ordinary Time

"Faithful Servant, Enter Your Master's Joy!"

* 1st reading: Proverbs 31
* Psalm: 128
* 2nd reading: 1 Thessalonians 5.1-6
* Gospel: Matthew 25.14-30

At the close of the liturgical year, the Church reflects on the consummation of world history, the coming of our Lord Jesus Christ in glory at the end of time. This theme spills over into the next year of grace, which begins with the Advent season.

Paul offered details on the technical term for Christ's "advent", the Parousia – and specific features of Christ's coming –in last Sunday's

Letter. This week, Paul reassures the Christians of Thessalonica that a believer's approach to the time of waiting for Christ's arrival is one of consolation, not anxiety. Christ will not surprise his disciples (as one might be startled by a thief coming in the night). When Jesus comes in glory, believers will be keeping watch in everyday life.

The Christian is to spend his or her lifetime "redeeming the time", engaged in making a solid contribution to family and society. This is the underlying challenge presented in both the reading from Proverbs, which describes the creative contribution women make, and in the gospel, where several men illustrate proper and improper use of God-given talents.

There are twenty-two letters in the Hebrew alphabet, and every one of the twenty-two verses of Proverbs 31.10-31 begins with a successive letter of the Hebrew alphabet. In other words, it is an acrostic (alphabetic) poem, artificial in format, much like the Shakespearean sonnet must have exactly fourteen lines.

This explains why the author seems to jump from theme to theme in describing the ideal (capable) wife; he is constrained by the letters of the alphabet he must use. The liturgical selection of ten of the twenty-two verses retains something of this arbitrary pattern in which the wife's virtues are listed.

The opening line – "a capable wife, who can find her?" – could suggest an impossible task. But an earlier verse on the good wife ("a good wife is the crown of her husband" [Proverbs 12.4]) hinted only that such a wife was a rarity. Once found, a capable wife is "far more precious than jewels", something also said of Wisdom ("She [Wisdom] is more precious than jewels, and nothing you desire can compare with her" [Proverbs 3.15]).

Whatever may have been true of the legal status of women in Israelite history, it seems there were always competent wives who took initiative in matters relating to the family fortune. In this they acted, as in this poem, with the full support of their husbands. The capable wife's endeavours fostered growth in the family's fortunes and so, as was recommended elsewhere in Proverbs, she came under the same obligation [as men] to be generous to the needy.

Quite appropriately, the poem ends with praise: first of the family to which she has contributed so much, then to her personal renown in particular ("let her works praise her in the city gates"). This anticipates the theme of praise given by the master to trustworthy servants in the gospel parable. Thus, industrious and trustworthy men and women receive commendation from the Word of God, the Lord of creation, and from Jesus himself, the full embodiment of Wisdom who teaches his disciples the way to salvation.

As an entrusted sum of money, the *talent* easily symbolized potential or one's capacity to achieve. Perhaps that is why Jesus chose it. A parable generally invites the hearer to imagine himself or herself in the role of one of the actors, challenged to reach the kind of decision the *dramatis personae* are called on to make.

The parable of the ten maidens prompted the listener to "be ready" because of a "coming". Today, disciples are asked to reflect on what readiness means concretely. Is it simply passively waiting (as the third slave thought)? Or is the time meant to be used responsibly with activities that the master on his return can approve (as the first and second slaves thought)?

The one-talent man was condemned for fearful inactivity. All hearers of the parable are challenged, by the two- and five-talent persons, to a dynamic and productive existence. Being "good and trustworthy" does not mean passivity as one waits for the Parousia of Christ, but a sense of creative responsibility that takes initiative, action and risks.

Thirty-Fourth Sunday in Ordinary Time

Christ the King
A Consistent Vision of Faith

* 1st reading: Ezekiel 34.11-12, 15-17
* Psalm: 23
* 2nd reading: 1 Corinthians 15.20-26, 28
* Gospel: Matthew 25.31-46

zekiel's ministry was to a people who had been driven into exile. They were refugees; they wondered whether God cared for them at all. God's answer was unambiguous: "I will seek out my sheep. I will rescue them from all the places to which they have been scattered on a day of clouds and thick darkness".

The prophet noted that God would "judge between one sheep and another, between rams and goats", underlining Ezekiel's frequent point that each person is responsible for his or her own activity in response to God's call. This point anticipates Jesus' criterion of judgment that "as you did [or did not do] it to one of the least of these brothers and sisters of mine, you did [or did not do] it to me".

Jesus' identification with others is an extraordinary aspect of his teaching. After the resurrection, he told Saul that he himself was one with the Church suffering persecution: "I am Jesus, whom you are persecuting" (Acts 9.5). In the majestic parable that closes his public teaching in Matthew, Jesus identified himself with the naked, hungry, thirsty, imprisoned, stranger and homeless.

Today, Jesus would doubtless associate himself with the drug addict, the bag lady, the refugee, the person with HIV/AIDS, the teenage runaway. As in the parable, there exists a real danger that people will not recognize him in them and, ignoring their needs, pass them and him by. People thereby risk losing their place in the kingdom, which God has "prepared for you from the foundation of the world".

Still, one should rejoice in the fact that the "eternal fire" of loss and separation from God was not prepared for human beings, but "for the devil and his angels". Those so preoccupied with self that they cannot see others' needs and minister to Jesus in them are the ones who should fear judgment.

Matthew lived in the era of the second generation of Christians, when the risk was great that the fervour of Christian discipleship would dissipate and the "love of many will grow cold" (Matthew 24.12). In Matthew's gospel, Christ constantly summons disciples to prove their love not merely in words but in deeds that reach out to others in service and love (cf. Matthew 5.16; 7.21-23).

ARCHBISHOP TERRENCE PRENDERGAST

Paul offered several descriptions of the end times – images that capture some aspect of Christ's role in, and the way believers will take part in, the fulfillment of God's saving plan. In today's letter, Paul points to the glorious victory that the Lord Jesus will one day achieve over the last enemy ranged against humanity: death.

At harvest time, the people of Israel offered to God the "first fruits" of all that the earth had produced, to symbolize their intent to consecrate the whole harvest. Just so, Christ is the "first fruits" of all believers who will share in that harvest of eternal life that God is gathering into the kingdom – the men, women and children led by the Good Shepherd.

As all men and women experience solidarity with Adam in sin – and in the sleep of death that sin brings – so all who, by faith, accept the gift of God's reconciling love possess solidarity with Jesus Christ. They will rise from death to everlasting life with him. God has "his own order" in bringing all of this about. In that "order", Christ serves as King until he can present all his subjects to the Father. Finally, God will be "all in all".

Christians pray that they may hear and heed the call of Christ the King as he comes to them in the needy of our day. In their response, disciples ask that God use them as instruments of his justice, that they share in and become heirs to "an eternal and universal kingdom: a kingdom of truth and life, a kingdom of holiness and grace, a kingdom of justice, love and peace" (from today's Preface).

In this way, the consistent vision of faith – which stretches from the prophets through Jesus to the Church of today – will continue to offer hope for orphan, widow, stranger and refugee. Through Christians – and others of goodwill – the kingdom vision moves ever closer to its consummation in history, to that day "when the Son of Man comes in his glory".

Transcontinental
PRINTING
IMPRIMERIE GAGNÉ

PRINTED IN CANADA